ROUTLEDGE LIBRARY EDITIONS:
LIBRARY AND INFORMATION SCIENCE

Volume 99

UNION CATALOGUES OF SERIALS

UNION CATALOGUES OF SERIALS
Guidelines for Creation and Maintenance,
with Recommended Standards for Bibliographic
and Holdings Control

JEAN WHIFFIN

LONDON AND NEW YORK

First published in 1983 by The Haworth Press, Inc.

This edition first published in 2020
by Routledge
2 Park Square, Milton Park, Abingdon, Oxon OX14 4RN

and by Routledge
52 Vanderbilt Avenue, New York, NY 10017

Routledge is an imprint of the Taylor & Francis Group, an informa business

© 1983 The Haworth Press, Inc.

All rights reserved. No part of this book may be reprinted or reproduced or utilised in any form or by any electronic, mechanical, or other means, now known or hereafter invented, including photocopying and recording, or in any information storage or retrieval system, without permission in writing from the publishers.

Trademark notice: Product or corporate names may be trademarks or registered trademarks, and are used only for identification and explanation without intent to infringe.

British Library Cataloguing in Publication Data
A catalogue record for this book is available from the British Library

ISBN: 978-0-367-34616-4 (Set)
ISBN: 978-0-429-34352-0 (Set) (ebk)
ISBN: 978-0-367-37187-6 (Volume 99) (hbk)
ISBN: 978-0-429-35301-7 (Volume 99) (ebk)

Publisher's Note
The publisher has gone to great lengths to ensure the quality of this reprint but points out that some imperfections in the original copies may be apparent.

Disclaimer
The publisher has made every effort to trace copyright holders and would welcome correspondence from those they have been unable to trace.

Union Catalogues of Serials
*Guidelines for Creation and Maintenance,
with Recommended Standards
for Bibliographic and Holdings Control*

Jean Whiffin

The Haworth Press
New York

Union Catalogues of Serials: Guidelines for Creation and Maintenance, with Recommended Standards for Bibliographic and Holdings Control has also been published as *The Serials Librarian,* Volume 8, Number 1, Fall 1983.

Copyright © 1983 by The Haworth Press, Inc. All rights reserved. Copies of articles in this publication may be reproduced noncommercially for the purpose of educational or scientific advancement. Otherwise, no part of this work may be reproduced or utilized in any form or by any means, electronic or mechanical including photocopying, microfilm and recording, or by any information storage and retrieval system without permission in writing from the publisher. Printed in the United States of America.

The Haworth Press, Inc., 28 East 22 Street, New York, NY 10010

Library of Congress Cataloging in Publication Data

Whiffin, Jean.
 Union catalogues of serials, guidelines for creation and maintenance, with recommended standards for bibliographic and holdings control.

 "Also. . .published as the Serials librarian, volume 8, number 1, fall 1983."
 Includes bibliographical references and index.
 1. Cataloging of serial publications—Standards. 2. Catalogs, Union—Standards. 3. Serials control systems—Standards. 4. Cataloging, Cooperative—Standards. I. Serials librarian. II. Title.
Z695.7.W47   1983   025.3'432   83-8586
ISBN 0-86656-238-9

Union Catalogues of Serials

Guidelines for Creation and Maintenance,
with Recommended Standards for Bibliographic
and Holdings Control

The Serials Librarian
Volume 8, Number 1

CONTENTS

Foreword	ix
Peter Gellatly	
Preface	xi
Jean Whiffin	
General Introduction	1

PART 1: GUIDELINES

Introduction	15
Chapter 1: General	17
Chapter 2: Functions	21
Chapter 3: Media Formats	27
Chapter 4: Scope	31
Chapter 5: Compilation	39
Chapter 6: Bibliographic Control	43
Chapter 7: Holdings Control	53
Chapter 8: Recommended Standards for Style, Presentation and Arrangement	63
Chapter 9: Criteria for Special Categories	71

Chapter 10: Responsibilities	83
Chapter 11: Output	87
Chapter 12: Relationships with Other Systems	89
References for Guidelines	95

PART 2: APPENDIXES

Appendix I: Definition of a Serial and Types of Serials	99
Appendix II: Glossary and Abbreviations	101
Appendix III: Summary of Essential Bibliographic and Holdings Data Elements	107

PART 3: SUPPLEMENT: LIST OF TITLES COVERED BY THE INTERNATIONAL SURVEY

Section 1: International Lists	111
Section 2: Other Lists, Arranged Alphabetically by Country of Location of the Contributing Libraries	117
Index	127

Foreword

The value of the union catalog is hard to exaggerate. Its primary purpose, the providing of access to materials not available locally, is so important that there is difficulty in imagining how libraries could function without it. But its importance is not limited to this one thing. The union catalog serves also to regularize and refine many other library activities, such as bibliographic control, collection management and network participation. The union catalog is a principal instrument of the practice of librarianship. It is of such consequence indeed that every librarian uses union catalogs in his or her daily work, and there are few who have not found themselves at one point or another engaged in the production of such works.

The compiling of union catalogs is itself one of the most purposeful and demanding activities of the librarian's working life. Yet until recently little attempt was made to standardize on other than a local level the arrangements that went into the making of union catalogs. There is, of course, the notable exception of the *ULS* and *NST*. The effort that produced these publications, one of the most effective cooperative ventures in international librarianship, required of participants a uniform style of reporting; and although the results obtained were sometimes less than satisfactory, the publications themselves were of unparalleled usefulness. They allowed libraries to work on a scale that previously was impossible for them or possible only at huge expense. Beyond this, they served notice of the potential that existed for larger and more meaningful kinds of cooperation in the future.

Most union catalogs are produced by single libraries or small groups of libraries working in concert; and thousands of such catalogs are still being produced. Each stands more or less by itself, although concessions are generally made to the requirements of AACR2, MARC and other regulatory presences. These catalogs, too, are highly useful, but inevitably they remain unique both in content and in shape and presentation of the entries of which they are composed.

While union catalogs, big and small, continue to appear, advances in electronics and telecommunications are giving impetus to notions concerning use of the union catalog in ways that until now have seemed impractical and visionary. Talk is heard, for instance, of its use in the promulgating of Universal Bibliographic Control and Universal Availability of Publications. And while it is true that both of these are far from realization, room exists to suppose that they are possible and perhaps in the end inevitable.

The need for common standards in union cataloging has always been recognized. The attempt to arrive at a form of practice with universal applicability is, however, new. Examples are found in ISBD, AACR2, MARC and CONSER of efforts to stretch bibliographic practice beyond national confines. The objective was never, of course, to produce worldwide acceptance of a single set of rules. Such an objective awaits definition. Indications are that the wait may not be long.

One such appears in the recent acceptance by Jean Whiffin of the University of Victoria, Canada, of an IFLA contract to prepare a proposal concerning the rationalization and standardization of union cataloging activities, as these are pursued on a world-wide scale.

We take great pleasure in presenting in this special issue of *The Serials Librarian,* Miss Whiffin's report to IFLA. It is expected that this report will form the basis of UNESCO/IFLA's standard for the compiling of union catalogs.

Peter Gellatly

Preface

The IFLA Section on Serial Publications, recognizing a strong need to establish international guidelines for the compilation of union catalogues/lists of serials, sponsored, with the financial assistance of UNESCO, a project to survey and analyse the existing bibliographic tools, and subsequently to formulate a code of good practice. The complete text of the first draft of the proposed new international standard is presented, preceded by a brief history of the project and its background. Reference is also made to some of the other recommendations emanating from the survey and from additional input contributed by over a hundred institutions and individuals during the course of the consultant's research.

Jean Whiffin

About the Author

Jean Whiffin is Head of the Serials Division, University of Victoria Library, Victoria, B.C., Canada V8W 3H5. She is a member of the Standing Committee of the IFLA Section on Serial Publications, and, since 1979, has been acting as consultant on union catalogues of serials to IFLA and UNESCO. The research for the draft international standard presented in this issue was partially funded by a contract between these two organizations.

Union Catalogues of Serials

*Guidelines for Creation and Maintenance,
with Recommended Standards
for Bibliographic and Holdings Control*

General Introduction

IFLA AND ITS OBJECTIVES

The International Federation of Library Associations and Institutions (IFLA) is a world-wide, independent, non-governmental association with over a thousand members in more than one hundred countries. Its basic objectives are:

—to promote international understanding, co-operation, discussion, research, and development, in all fields of library and information service activity;
—to promote the continuing education of personnel;
—to provide a body through which librarianship can be represented in matters of international interest.

The organization works through two kinds of unit: 1) the Divisions, Sections, and Round Tables; 2) the International Offices and Programmes. It also co-operates with other organizations, both inter-governmental and non-governmental, to pursue its objectives, particularly the United Nations Educational, Scientific and Cultural Organization (UNESCO), to achieve the aims of both bodies for the development of libraries and librarianship. IFLA shares its experiences with UNESCO, keeps UNESCO aware of its programmes and activities, and seeks moral and financial support for their execution, wherever appropriate, from UNESCO.

The Sections are the basic professional units of IFLA. Each Section proposes its own programmes, but these are reviewed by a Co-ordinating Board consisting of the elected officers of all Sections in a given Division, of which there are seven. The Divisions' programmes are reviewed by the Professional Board, which consists of one officer from each Division. The Section on Serial Publications exists to study the problems of handling serials in libraries, including bibliographic control, management, and conservation. It is one of five sections belonging to the Division of Collections and Services.

THE UNESCO/IFLA UNION LIST PROJECT AND ITS BACKGROUND

During the Open Session of the Section on Serial Publications at the 1978 IFLA annual conference in Czechoslovakia, a resolution was passed expressing strong need for the establishment of international guidelines for union lists of serials and suggesting to the Professional Board that such a project was very much within the spirit of the Universal Availability of Publications (UAP) Programme. The objective of this major IFLA programme is the widest possible availability of published material to intending users, wherever and whenever they need it, as an essential element in economic, social, educational and personal development. The programme aims to improve availability at all levels from the local to the international, and at all stages from the publication of new material to the retention of last copies, and to ensure that improved access to information in published materials is matched by improved access to the materials themselves. The usefulness of union catalogues and lists of serials as registers of existing serial resources, as the means of achieving physical access to these resources through the location information provided, and as showing the state of preservation of serial literature, serves to emphasize the relevance of the Section's project to the UAP programme. The incentive provided at the 1978 annual meeting eventually led to financial support from UNESCO for a research study to determine guidelines for the compilation of union catalogues and lists of serials. Mr. Ross Bourne, the Section's Chairman, undertook to direct the project, and Miss Jean Whiffin, a personal member of the Section and an observer on its Standing Committee, accepted an invitation to carry out the research and preparatory work to establish draft guidelines.

It was the expectation of the Section that the end-product of the work it had commissioned would contribute to needed standardization and compatibility of serials control across national boundaries, as well as improve access to serial collections, thus furthering not only the UAP concept, but also another IFLA special programme—Universal Bibliographic Control (UBC). This programme aims to eliminate multiplication of effort in bibliographic recording and provide records which are internationally standardized, internationally compatible, and internationally available.

The project was undertaken during a period of both technological and bibliographic change. Although printed union lists were still preponderant, microfiche was becoming a very common medium, while on-line services were beginning to increase rapidly. Touch-sensitive terminals in libraries and computers in the home figured among many technological developments which were revolutionizing the means and the place of access to information. The first steps were taken to see that automated library systems interface with outside information systems, and planning commenced for Open Systems Interconnection (OSI). AACR.2 was implemented by the national libraries in the U.K., the U.S., Canada and Australia, among others, but, in spite of the many improvements in this new cataloguing code, it left several problems unresolved in respect of serials management systems and union catalogues of serials. A number of potential "master" serials data bases already existed to which holdings could be attached, including the CONSER project, the files of the International Serials Data System (ISDS), of some commercial firms publishing serial directories, and of some of the indexing and abstracting services. Several bibliographic utilities began to offer union list capabilities.

In spite of all this flurry of activity on both the technological and the bibliographic front, the signs were not encouraging. Traditional editorial principles which create order out of chaos where variant cataloguing standards are involved were being ignored in many machine-readable union catalogues, and the need for editorial work on holdings statements is not always appreciated. There was an imbalance between the attention paid to the standardization of bibliographic descriptions and that of holdings statements. Lack of standards for the latter was resulting in a proliferation of non-standardized data in most computer-produced serials lists and wide diversity in the way the same sorts of information were being handled. The number of organizations and institutions, including the American National Standards Institute (ANSI), the British Standards Institution (BSI), the CONSER project, and the Canadian Union Catalogue Task Group, which had been or were attempting to standardize specifications for serials holdings statements and define minimum reporting levels pointed to a need to suggest international guidelines before new problems were created by the multiplication and incompatibility of national holdings standards, and augmented the inconsistency on the bibliographic scene. The time had come to make the most of opportunities provided by computerized production in both the developed and developing countries, and to share records if agreed-upon standards were followed, but lack of standardization in both bibliographic and holdings data constituted a major barrier to effective use of union catalogues/lists, and some technically advanced systems were already producing tools which were less valuable than their so-called primitive predecessors. The situation could only be worsened by linkages among systems and transfer of data from one system to another without human review. The need for international guidelines was not only strong, but urgent.

METHODOLOGY

A two-step project had been envisaged by the Section on Serial Publications, comprising a survey of 200 existing union catalogues and lists (print, microform and on-line), to collect information as a basis on which to analyse and evaluate the data elements adopted and the record structure, followed by the formulation of guidelines for future compilers.

The Section developed a framework for the analysis and evaluation phase, but alternative suggestions for the holdings data were presented by the consultant and approved at the next annual meeting in Copenhagen in 1979. The hope was expressed that this part of the project would eventually contribute to standardizing specifications and to defining minimum reporting standards for worthwhile utilization of the information at local, regional, national, and international levels, thus reducing the frustrations experienced by interlending personnel, the primary users of union catalogues/lists of serials, and acquisitions librarians, for whom this facet is almost equally important.

The final framework therefore encompassed 19 bibliographic and 14 holdings characteristics. These were as follows:-

Bibliographic characteristics

—Type of publication
—Method of up-dating
—Physical format
—Function
—Geographic coverage
—Type of contributing library
—Current/retrospective coverage
—Bibliographic completeness
—Policy on title changes
—Subject
—Language coverage
—Area coverage
—Period coverage
—Type of serial covered
—Arrangement
—Aids to user
—On-line systems access points and services
—Method of compilation
—Special features

Holdings characteristics

—General data
—Institutional identification
—Holdings strings
—Copy data
—Holdings notation:-
 —system
 —completeness indicator

  —current acquisition status indicator
  —type of notation
  —retention data
  —microform data
—Local control data
—Lending and photocopying policy
—Prefixes
—Special features

For the survey phase, the consultant was required to make a selection representative of union lists of all types, both well known and less well known, with 25 to 30 per cent consisting of titles from the developing countries. An intensive literature search was conducted in the Fall of 1979. Special appeals were made for material to be sent for examination, and research was undertaken at the national libraries in Canada, the U.S., and the U.K. Comments and suggestions were invited from users of union catalogues and lists of serials to learn their expectations and needs for this kind of tool, their views on the strengths and weaknesses of the ones they regularly consult, and their specifications for the ideal model, as well as from editors, who were requested to send written policies and other documentation regarding bibliographic and holdings standards followed, compilation methodology, instructions to participants, etc. It was also deemed advisable by the consultant to advertise the project widely, to avoid the type of criticism which had occurred in the past following some other international attempts at standardization with wide ramifications.

The world-wide interest shown in the project was most encouraging. One hundred and nineteen institutions, agencies and individuals sent in contributions and suggestions. Some of them, particularly in the developing countries, wrote several times asking for progress reports, newsletters, bulletins to act as a forum for the exchange of ideas, and, of course, the draft of the *Guidelines,* which was wanted "yesterday". The reaction confirmed the worthwhile and timely nature of this attempt to bring about greater and international standardization of a type of library tool essential for successful resource-sharing of serial publications. It also resulted in the consultant being inundated with material to be analysed, interpreted, synthesized and output in an intelligent form for consumption!

The major literature on the subject was also reviewed, and discussions were held with interlending, union catalogue, and serials librarians during the consultant's travels, to provide another form of input.

All titles were examined as a whole, not just sample pages and the introduction. Approximately 25 per cent of them proved to be international in respect of the basis of co-operation, further emphasizing the need for standardization across national boundaries. The other 75 per cent exemplified all types of union catalogue/list activity in 60 different countries. It is believed that there has been no previous survey of this type of bibliographic tool of comparable breadth and depth.

The consultant was also required to evaluate each title analysed and assess its degree of success in terms of its particular purpose. Evaluation proved difficult, as the function is not always specified by the editors, while union lists frequently serve purposes beyond those actually specified. Some lists which proved very successful at the time of initial publication may be less satisfactory in present-day perspective. The historical-bibliography type may increase or decrease in value as time passes. The use of a list within the country of publication and in other countries as a "foreign" publication is not necessarily the same. In the last resort, only the user himself can decide its value for his particular purpose.

Evaluation criteria were drawn up for the various types of union lists, including local, regional, national, subject, newspapers, historical bibliographies, microform, and on-line systems. An attempt was made to estimate the strengths and weaknesses of each title surveyed, and ratings were assigned in respect of success in terms of specified purpose. A rating was also given to those facets which, in the consultant's judgment, represent the essentials for optimal inter-library-loan use.

In the Winter of 1980 and the Spring of 1981, the consultant completed the initial project by analysing the survey data collected on the worksheets and selecting the essential elements from the representatives of all types of union catalogues/lists. Similarities were identified and those features which characterize the more successful titles presented as examples of good practice, but the literature review, input from all sources, and standardization in related areas, were also taken into account. The "distilled essence", namely the first draft (June 1981) of *Guidelines for Union Catalogues of Serials,* was formally presented to the IFLA Section on Serial Publications at its annual meeting in Leipzig in August 1981, together with a number of recommendations arising from the project. The full text of the *Guidelines* in the consultant's first draft immediately follows this special introduction. It is accompanied by a supplement which lists the two hundred titles covered by the international survey.

THE END-PRODUCT

Within these Guidelines the consultant tried to do the following:-

—To re-define the functions of union catalogues/lists in the light of the survey findings and of changes resulting from technological developments, and to reflect the state of the art.
—To identify the principles and standards which are still valid from the past while anticipating those needed for the immediate future.

—To compare the merits of various formats.
—To look at the area of contribution to a union catalogue/list in its relevance to an hierarchical national lending system and the UAP Programme.
—To consider the factors to be borne in mind in using machine-readable records from various sources.
—To suggest what she believes to be:-
   (a) the needed uniformity of cataloguing practices, together with a minimum bibliographic data element set;
   (b) the needed uniformity of holdings control, together with a minimum holdings data element set.
—To provide standards for style, presentation and arrangement.
—To provide criteria for special categories, such as newspapers, microfiche editions, and on-line services.
—To cope with the needs drawn to her attention, from the time the union catalogue/list is only a gleam in someone's eye to the moment the finished product is deposited in a national bibliographic agency.
—To situate this kind of tool in relation to other types of serial control systems, and within the broader context of the information transfer chain.

A standard acquires its mandate either by following or leading, either by reflecting the consensus or by demanding improvement. The consultant endeavoured to do both by describing what is characteristic of union catalogues/lists throughout the world, but where it was clear that a better state of affairs was needed, she had no hesitation in prescribing what she believed to be the minimum essential. As mentioned in the introduction to the *Guidelines,* the goal has been to present the practical optimum for design, compilation and maintenance.

SURVEY RESULTS AND RECOMMENDATIONS

It is hoped that the detailed findings of the international survey can be published at a future date. It is only possible now to mention a few highlights and the major recommendations.

The consultant was required to advise on the adequate use of the national and international files of the International Serials Data System in the preparation of a union list, but the survey provided insufficient information. Many of the titles examined predated the few years during which this data base has been available. International Standard Serial Numbers (ISSNs) are now being displayed in many instances, but there was no evidence of the use of the ISDS bibliographic files to create a union catalogue/list of serials beyond the FINUC-S (Finnish Union Catalogue-Serials) and NOSP (Nordisk Samkatalog över Periodica—Union Catalogue of Serials in Nordic Research Libraries) projects. Documentation reviewed indicated that the lack of bibliographic data and ISSNs for retrospective titles already included in union lists, and of a one-to-one correspondence between records created according to the ISDS standard and AACR in respect of the definition of a discrete bibliographic unit, the problems with the harmonization of national library and ISDS cataloguing, difficulties in correcting errors in ISDS material, and backlogs in assigning ISSNs, all at present constitute stumbling-blocks to greater utilization of the files of this international network. However, the multiple functions which union catalogues/lists can and do successfully serve, even though 99 per cent of the titles surveyed utilized only brief bibliographic information, once again brings into question the value, for *serials* cataloguing, of full bibliographic entries to the International Standard Bibliographic Description (ISBD) level, leaving aside its weaknesses in respect of older serials and the general problems of describing a constantly moving object.

It was also anticipated that the consultant would be able to draw up a generalized compilation methodology, but it was found that the many variables involved precluded such a formulation, as explained in section 5.1 of the *Guidelines*.

The state of the art of recording and displaying holdings data can be summarized in one word—chaos. Such standardization as does exist, e.g., in institutional identification symbols, is flying out of the window as bibliographic utilities "do their own thing". Libraries are entering holdings directly into central data bases without the editorial control which existed hitherto in the best-quality traditional union lists. There would appear to be little appreciation, outside the special union catalogue offices in the major national libraries and bibliographic agencies, of the many functions which meaningfully collocated specific holdings statements can perform for a wide range of users, including interlending personnel, scholars wishing to consult material in other libraries, collection-builders, and anyone attempting to preserve rare or deteriorating serial files through the integration of different sets to gather a complete run for reproduction, or assembling one good file and discarding the duplicates in a co-operative acquisition programme. Problem identification and sound decision-making are just as needed in holdings control as they are in bibliographic control, and demand the attention of suitably-trained and knowledgeable personnel in both individual institutions contributing to union catalogues and in the editorial office which sets the standards and sees they are consistently applied, if communication of this kind of information is to be improved.

This complex and wide-ranging project served to draw attention to a number of related matters requiring study and resolution, not only in serials control but in the field of information control, and the consultant presented several recommendations to the IFLA Section on Serial Publications in 1981, along with the first draft of the *Guidelines*. One concerned the use of the generic term "union list". It was found that it is less prevalent than "union catalogue" (or its equivalent in other languages) or other descriptions, while its use often results in simple title listings without adequate bibliographic identification to perform even the most basic functions. Moreover, the term "union list" is becoming obsolescent in the on-line environment, since it implies a printed product. Hence "union catalogue" was recommended as the preferred generic term.

The following constitute the consultant's principal recommendations to the IFLA Section on Serial Publications:-

- The minimum set of data elements for bibliographic and holdings control provided in the first draft of the *Guidelines* dated June 1981 should be adopted by the Section as the international standard for union catalogues of serials.
- The Section's Working Group on Union Catalogues of Serials should be enlarged to include more librarians with substantial experience in serials management systems and union catalogues of serials, in order to carry forward the recommendations, pursue the required standards more expeditiously, and distribute the burden of work still to be undertaken.
- The Section's Working Group on Newspapers should be enlarged to include more experts on bibliographic control of newspapers, particularly with experience in compiling union catalogues of newspapers.
- The Section should take appropriate steps to seek an ISO (International Organization for Standardization) standard for serials holdings statements at the summarized condensed level.
- The Section should encourage the development of an international standard for institutional identification codes, and should make submissions to appropriate standardizing bodies.
- The Section should ask for representation on the Common Communication Format working group, in order to see this format is extended to include the data elements needed for union catalogues of serials.
- The Section should set up a special study group to examine improvements needed in multi-national cataloguing codes and in the *Guidelines for ISDS* in respect of newspapers, and all serials in microform or other reproduction, with particular reference to the use of the bibliographic records in serials management systems and union catalogues of serials.

—UNESCO should be asked to provide the necessary funds to enable one of the developing countries to create a union catalogue of serials, using the principles and standards outlined in the first draft of the *Guidelines* dated June 1981, to test their validity for general use in the developing countries.

—Funds should be sought to prepare a handbook for use in the developing countries, and countries without a national bibliographic agency, covering the various types of serial control systems and their relationships, and to assist these countries in compiling, or contributing to, union catalogues of serials.

—The Section should make a submission to the ISO groups working on micrographics standards, particularly in respect of the bibliographic information for headers in microfiche editions of union catalogues of serials.

—Ways and means should be explored of stepping-up the programme for the assignment of ISSNs to titles published prior to 1960.

—The Section should give consideration to the preparation of a standardized input form for use by institutions contributing to a union catalogue of serials.

—The Section should draw the attention of national bibliographic agencies to the necessity for the stipulations for legal deposit of publications of the national imprint to include new and revised print and microfiche editions of union catalogues of serials.

—The Section should encourage the setting-up of clearinghouses to collect and disseminate information about union catalogue of serials activities, to share expertise and knowledge of new standards, techniques and methods, and to promote communication and co-ordination among union catalogue of serials agencies.

These and other recommendations were subsequently referred to the Section's Working Group on Union Catalogues of Serials, which was expanded, as the consultant had suggested, and comprises, at the time of writing: Marjorie Bloss (U.S.), Ross Bourne (U.K.), Günter Franzmeier (Federal Republic of Germany), Erica Ljungdahl (Sweden) and Jean Whiffin (Canada).

FUTURE OF THE GUIDELINES

Following presentation at the 1981 IFLA annual meeting, the *Guidelines* were distributed for review and comment by members of the Section, the Directors of the ISDS Centres, and contributors to the project.

At the time of writing of this paper (Summer 1982), an international panel of experts, comprising representatives of the ISDS International

Centre, the IFLA International Offices for UBC and UAP, the Nordisk Samkatalog över Periodica (NOSP) Project, the Secretary of the IFLA Section on Serial Publications, and the consultant, was reviewing the first draft and the comments received, in preparation for a final version to be published in the UNESCO guidelines series.

Part 1

GUIDELINES

Introduction

These *Guidelines* present codes of good practice, and recommended standards for bibliographic and holdings control, to be used in the creation and maintenance of union catalogues of serials, bearing in mind the requirements for international exchange. They are intended:

(a) to have universal relevance to all countries:

—in improving physical and bibliographic access to serials resources, thus removing some of the barriers to effective utilization and preservation;
—in making the most of opportunities provided by computerized production, while ensuring the traditional principles and recognized standards are maintained in effecting the change from manual to more sophisticated automated systems;

(b) to give practical guidance on:

—the components in the preparation and production of a union catalogue of serials, with consideration of all pertinent standards;
—the administrative machinery required to bring each project to fruition (i.e., the role and function of both the editing agency and the participating institutions, and the underlying principles of cooperation);
—the interface with other serials control systems and other information networks.

These *Guidelines* have been prepared taking into account the analysis and evaluation of two hundred printed, microfiche and on-line union catalogues of serials of all kinds, in a world-wide survey carried out in 1980, on behalf of the IFLA Section on Serial Publications, by Jean Whiffin of the University of Victoria Library, Canada, and the contributions she received from over a hundred institutions and individuals, as well as a literature review and a reassessment of the functions in an era of rapid technological change.

It is anticipated that the *Guidelines,* in presenting the practical optimum for design, compilation and maintenance, and in setting out the functions which such a tool can perform when prepared according to the recommended standards for bibliographic and holdings control, will have particular value for networks, bibliographic agencies, and institutions planning the establishment of a new, or the improvement of an existing, union catalogue of serials. In countries with long-established traditions of compiling such tools, the *Guidelines* may suggest practical ways to upgrade the coverage, contents and presentation, whether in print, microfiche or on-line, while drawing attention to areas in which standardization has not yet been achieved, or will be required in the future to ensure compatibility of serials control across national boundaries and to meet the challenge of Open Systems Interconnection.

Chapter 1

General

1 The type of bibliographic tool for which guidelines are provided in this publication is most frequently described generically as either a "union list" or a "union catalogue". Since use of the word "list" in the past has often resulted in the production of tools with inadequate bibliographic detail to perform even the basic functions, and since this term itself is becoming obsolete in the automated environment, the description union *catalogue* is to be preferred, and is used consistently throughout these guidelines.

1.1 *DEFINITIONS*

1.1.1 A *serial* is a publication in print or in non-print form, issued in successive parts, usually having numerical or chronological designations, and intended to be continued indefinitely. Serials include periodicals, newspapers, annuals (reports, yearbooks, directories, etc.), journals, memoirs, proceedings, transactions etc. of societies, and monographic series.

1.1.2 A *union catalogue of serials* is a catalogue provided through the medium of print, microform, or visual display, which gives, in one or more orders of arrangement, appended to one bibliographic record for each discrete serial item, the location and summarized holdings data concerning two or more participating institutions.

This term is not normally used for the serials catalogue of a single institution. But large single administrative systems with multiple major branches in widely-spread locations, or with major separate collections each with its own identity, may provide their users with a union catalogue. Single institutions with multiple service-points of this nature are therefore covered by these guidelines, as well as local, regional, national, and international, union catalogues of serials.

1.2 UNDERLYING PRINCIPLES OF CO-OPERATION

The concept of sharing of serials and of information about serials is implicit in the rationale for a union catalogue. It is essentially a co-operative venture, and one which requires planning and co-ordination to achieve its objectives.

1.2.1 A *Project Director* should be appointed to plan, organize, and manage the union catalogue of serials. The needs of participating institutions should be determined, and a well-defined and realistic goal should be set. It is advisable that the user-group in view consist of institutions with interests in common and prepared to share their serial resources.

All possibilities should be explored to ensure there is no duplication of existing work, either in creating the data base or in requesting participants to contribute holdings. Without careful planning, union catalogues can create further problems through proliferation and incompatibility. Consideration should be given to using existing bibliographic data banks and the techniques and experience of other union catalogue staff, particularly in national bibliographic agencies. Nor should computer programmes be written without due investigation of the suitability of an existing software package. Some bibliographic utilities now offer a capability to maintain union catalogues on-line.

Users of computerized files should seek a system which can handle both successive-entry and latest-title output, and accommodate all title and issuing-body approaches. Records should be translatable into a common national MARC-Serials format, thus ensuring international compatibility and exchange.

1.2.2 Particular attention should be paid to securing suitably qualified serials librarians as editors, the necessary bibliographic and technical resources and facilities to produce the union catalogue, and to ensuring that adequate funding is available for all phases of the project, including continuation by frequently-published new editions.

1.2.3 The Project Director should seek the co-operation of all suitable centres and libraries with strong serials collections, with trained personnel to contribute to the union catalogue, and willing to make their resources accessible. An appropriate spread and mixture of libraries throughout the area of contribution should be sought from the outset, with special attention paid to securing the participation of smaller public and special libraries with resources which might be made available on a wider basis through interlending and co-operative acquisition agreements within the defined scope of the project. Certain categories, e.g. newspapers, require the active co-operation of non-institutional contributors, such as publishing houses, and may benefit from including the holdings of private libraries.

1.3 The *editorial staff* should consist of experienced and dedicated serials librarians with a thorough understanding of the theory and practice of serials control. This team should possess both a fine appreciation of the many functions a high-quality union catalogue can perform, and a realization of the importance of all appropriate serials standards, particularly the use of the International Standard Serial Number (ISSN), described in 6.1.4.

1.4 The responsibilities of editors and contributors are outlined in Chapter 10.

1.5 While the sponsor and publisher of the union catalogue of serials may inspire the confidence of users and provide some guide to its quality, it must always be borne in mind that this kind of bibliographic tool is a co-operative venture requiring firm co-ordination, and that therefore the quality of the resulting product will depend on the editors, the information contributed, and the level and strength of pressure exerted to conform to the standards set.

Chapter 2
Functions

2 Traditionally, union catalogues of serials have performed identification and location functions, to facilitate interlending and collection-rationalization processes.[1] As their number and variety have increased, they have come to serve other important functions. Technological developments, particularly in telecommunications, allowing correlation and duplication of data bases with improved access and response, are extending traditional functions, which nonetheless remain valid even in an era of transition. It is anticipated that union catalogues of serials will undergird the electronic location and delivery systems of the future, as they have supported simpler structures in the past, and will continue to respond to the serials information requirements of librarians, archivists, documentalists, serials suppliers, students, scholars and researchers in all fields of knowledge.

This Chapter outlines the multiple functions which a union catalogue of serials can serve, provided bibliographic and holdings data are integrated, meet the minimum standards specified in Chapters 6 and 7, and are gathered together and displayed in meaningful collocation.

2.1 *GUIDE FOR SERIALS COLLECTION DEVELOPMENT*

A union catalogue of serials is a *register of existing serial resources* in a given area, and it provides the first and most essential stage of making maximum use of such collections. It is a *tool for orderly collection development and rationalization,* at both the *title* level and the *volumes or issues* level, and reveals strengths and weaknesses. It supports selection and deselection decisions, furthers co-operative acquisition and specialization schemes, and prevents unnecessary duplication while indicating potential for enrichment of area resources.

Comparison and evaluation of specific holdings statements

not only show lacunae in files, and help to avoid duplication of retrospective volumes, but also enable collections to be reorganized, through consolidation of broken sets into fewer (and more complete) files, and disposal of unwanted materials by weeding, exchange, sale, or transfer to a regional storage centre.

2.2 LOCATION GUIDE PROVIDING PHYSICAL ACCESS TO SERIAL COLLECTIONS

A union catalogue of serials is a *location device and means of achieving physical access to serial collections.* It is the basic ingredient of a successful search, through the provision of appropriate identification in a single serial entry which gathers together information regarding availability of many years of individual issues and articles distributed in the collections of participating institutions.

It is an essential tool for *interlending* purposes, showing which location offers the greatest certainty of success to borrow or photocopy needed material, and specifically the *nearest* holding institution for speed of service to the patron. It provides access to an hierarchical lending system based on existing distributed collections, which exhausts *local* resources first, and makes serial literature, wherever held, available through a linked bibliographic network.

It is equally important as an essential tool enabling the user, through the provision of a wide range of specific statements indicating any incompleteness, to evaluate the extent of holdings in the maximum number of locations for *on-site consultation* purposes, whether he wishes to examine one particular issue, multiple issues or multiple titles; or follow data through each volume of one file; or compare all variants of a given issue to solve bibliographic problems of origin, history and text; or browse in titles not covered by indexing and abstracting services.

Union catalogues of serials thus offer a more efficient and less expensive alternative to setting up centralized serials lending collections, because they access and use *existing* serials resources, *both current and retrospective,* without additional buildings and duplication of files, and answer the needs of patrons who wish to consult serials as well as those who wish to borrow or photocopy individual articles.

The union catalogue of serials constitutes a major component of the *Universal Availability of Publications* programme. The total serials collections of a nation can be made available to each individual patron in whatever institution he may be using as his base, through the dissemination of holdings data and their co-operative exploitation in a national resource network. It is of prime importance in all areas which need to pool their resources, particularly in the developing countries, and may be said to be the key to enrichment of library opportunity in respect of serial literature.

2.3 *INSTRUMENT OF PRESERVATION OF SERIAL LITERATURE*

A union catalogue of serials is an *inventory* of the serial collections of two or more participating institutions, which, by the use of specific holdings and retention statements, shows the state of *preservation* of serial literature. It may serve as an inventory of the serial resources of a nation, or of serials of the national imprint.

It reveals holdings of early and other rare serials and is particularly useful as an inventory of extant volumes and issues of material depleted through wars or natural disasters, or subject to rapid physical deterioration (such as newsprint), or otherwise vulnerable to loss. It may assist serials acquisitions librarians to determine what constitutes a complete file of a given title, or assess the rarity of a file.

Information concerning the preservation of *national imprints* is of vital importance when the material is no longer extant in the country of origin, or is only available in that area, or is dispersed in collections other than those of the national bibliographic agency, or is held only in libraries of a country once linked through politics, history or language.

The preservation function is extended when the union catalogue of serials collocates originals, reprints and microforms. The state of *substitution programmes* is shown, and a register of replacements in existence or being undertaken is provided. The union catalogue of serials also supplies the necessary information to prevent duplication of filming and reprint projects, and encourages new co-operative preservation programmes by showing the possibilities of integrating files to gather the most complete run for reproduction.

In the case of *newspapers,* the inventory and preservation function is paramount.

2.4 SOURCE OF BIBLIOGRAPHIC DATA FOR SERIALS

The union catalogue of serials is a source for the *identification and verification* of serial publications, through the provision of a set of data elements unique to this type of tool. It enables the user to identify unambiguously a serial for which he has a precise citation, or for which he knows one of the titles, one of the issuing bodies, or the ISSN. It thus provides *bibliographic access to serial collections.*

It serves as a source of *cataloguing data* for all library departments, but particularly for reference and serials librarians. The bibliographic data may also provide the core of a simple serials management system or be used as a replacement for, or supplement to, cataloguing activities at the institutional level. The union catalogue of serials supplies the most essential data to trace the publishing history of each serial. It is particularly useful for information on new and recently-changed titles, and those published prior to legal deposit, since these are not necessarily included in national bibliographies. It thus helps to solve the complex problems of *better bibliographic control over the world's serial literature.*

A new dimension is available in the on-line environment, since this permits distributed access. The union catalogue of serials can not only serve as a source of cataloguing data, but provide a *context for the creation of new cataloguing,* allowing the logical integration of serials records emanating from a variety of sources.

2.5 BIBLIOGRAPHY OF SERIAL LITERATURE

The union catalogue of serials may constitue a *major bibliography* in its own right (or provide one as a by-product), for a type of serial, a format, a period, a region, etc. In the case of *newspapers,* it is often the only bibliography.

If there is no national bibliography, it may serve as the serials component. As indicated above, it may include serials which precede the publication of the national bibliography, or supplement the latter by covering serials omitted therefrom, or up-date information therein in respect of changes of all kinds. By discovering, identifying and recording domestic serials. the union catalogue is a *means of achieving current and retrospective bibliographic control of serials of the national imprint.*

2.6   *NODE IN A SERIALS NETWORK*

The union catalogue of serials may serve as a *node in an hierarchical lending system,* and this function is now being extended in an era of rapid technological development.

When a union catalogue of serials operates in a linked environment through electronic interconnection it provides the possibilities of:

(a) dynamic serials data exchange;
(b) file building;
(c) dynamic access to other serials data bases; and
(d) automatic routing of an inter-library-loan request from the network of origin, to another network's on-line catalogue, to the holding institution.

It therefore functions as a *clearing-house* or *switching centre.* It ties libraries together and places them in the framework of a larger access system. Separate serials data bases can be linked by a sophisticated telecommunications network to form a confederation of union catalogues. The user searches the literature for serials citations, determines whether the information exists, in what form, and where, through use of a union catalogue of serials, which then leads into linked searching. If the system embodies a document-ordering module, then the information chain is complete. Serial material has been acquired, recorded and catalogued in individual libraries, which have contributed holdings data to the centre of a co-operative enterprise, where a tool has been established to provide access, through referral, to appropriate resources, and which permits the user to generate on-line an inter-library-loan request or order for the actual document required.

It is expected that, in future, this function of union catalogues will be even further extended as the inventory and location information they contain is passed against the data bases of the indexing and abstracting services. Through automated use of these services, an article designated through a completed search will be automatically linked to the closest holding location to produce the loan request or the document order.

The International Standard Serial Number will play an increasingly important role in such linkages.

2.7   The above functions may be said to constitute the optimal maximum. It is recognized that, for many countries, the union catalogue of serials will continue to serve primarily as an instrument for interlending and collection rationalization. Use of the minimum data elements for printed and fiche editions, within the context of the general principles recommended in these *Guidelines,* should enable union catalogues of serials produced in the developing countries to perform the traditional functions successfully, while remaining compatible with the systems of other libraries which have reached a more advanced stage of technological development of information facilities.

In all countries, the union catalogue of serials provides an *instrument for more effective utilization of serials resources.*

Chapter 3
Media Formats

3 Union catalogues of serials may be produced in print or in microform or displayed on screens which are part of computer terminals or video systems, or made available in any combination of the three media.

3.1 *THE UNION CATALOGUE OF SERIALS IN PRINTED FORM*

Print format is the easiest to use and requires no special equipment. It offers convenience of handling and carrying and makes use of a universal medium (paper). Provided a suitable introduction is included, this format can be used by even unsophisticated library patrons without further intermediary. It is not, however, easy to up-date unless computerized, and even then may be an expensive proposition in respect of frequent new editions and cumulations because of high costs of paper, printing and distribution.

3.2 *THE UNION CATALOGUE OF SERIALS IN MICROFORM*

Computer-output-microform (COM), particularly *microfiche,* offers a cheaper and more compact output and distribution medium. It is faster to produce and easier to up-date. Since multiple copies can be produced inexpensively, wider distribution is possible and this, in turn, leads to greater use of library resources. It extends the usefulness of a union catalogue of serials already in print. But microfiche is slower to access than printed copy, and does require a greater level of sophistication in the patron. User instruction may be necessary in handling, loading and accessing the fiche. Good quality reader-printers (preferably with dual carriers) should be provided and regularly maintained at multiple viewing stations to prevent user queuing.

Microfiche is not recommended for *continuous* daily use in interlending offices and in other heavy use areas because of physical problems, particularly visual, in locating information in microform.

3.3 *THE UNION CATALOGUE OF SERIALS IN ON-LINE DISPLAY SYSTEMS*

On-line systems offer four major advantages:-

(1) They are more user-oriented because all access points are linked to a master bibliographic record and all are equally valid and retrievable.

(2) They provide a data base for inter-library-loan and other traditional union catalogue of serials functions, with the added flexibility of multiple search, print and display options, and can serve different functions by reorganizing or accessing a single file in a variety of ways.

(3) They make the typing, editing and frequent up-dating of serial bibliographic and holdings information both faster and easier, and consequently represent the most efficient method for preparing and maintaining a union catalogue of serials.

(4) They make this up-to-date information available directly, instantaneously and simultaneously, in multiple disparate locations.

Such systems do, however, represent a significant investment in installation, hardware and software maintenance, communications costs, and allowing for a back-up in the case of power outages, equipment breakdown, or deficiencies in vendor services.

3.3.1 Due attention must also be paid to the health, safety and psychological factors involved. Frequent changes of shift are necessary for data input operators, and work-stations must be set up in such a way as to minimize the effects of unsatisfactory angling of screens, flickering, heat from tubes, and fluorescent glare. Government standards should be scrupulously followed to avoid potential radiation hazards. For the same reasons, on-line systems are not recommended for *continuous* daily use in inter-library-loan and other heavy use areas.

3.3.2 Rapid and easy consultation is as important in on-line systems as in printed. Effective use of terminals is directly related to the ability of users, and the realization that information is a resource which needs to be facile of access. Over-sophistication in access and over-supply of information can create problems for users. Advanced technological systems are only of value to the library patron if he obtains the same or greater satisfaction from them as he did in earlier manual systems.

While librarians now intervene between the patron and the computer, direct patron interface with serials data bases should be anticipated, both for access to catalogue records and inter-library direct user access. Patrons with a precise title can already use efficiently some on-line union catalogues of serials, find their location, and then use an on-line document ordering system to obtain their inter-library-loan item. The advent of user-friendly terminals, interaction with the computer in tutorial, questionnaire or command mode, touch-sensitive screens, and voice-activated searches, will dramatically change previous librarian-patron relationships. Eventually the user will be able to have the information available to him in his own home via cable television or a personal computer.

Creators of on-line union catalogues of serials should therefore be preparing for the average user's approach to electronic bibliographic access by giving help in terminal operation, developing systems which can be more easily used by the inexperienced or casual system patron, creating unambiguous command language, simplifying the formulation of enquiries, and generally providing instruction which can be tuned to the level of sophistication of the user.

3.4 A combination of an on-line system, with microfiche back-up in frequent editions, and a printed version occasionally, is recommended for all but the most comprehensive systems, for which a printed union catalogue may be prohibitively expensive.

Whether a manual or machine-readable system is utilized, it cannot be over-emphasized that adherence to the traditional principles of creating union catalogues of serials is essential. A computerized system which fails to communicate is less useful that a manual one which does.

3.5 *UP-DATING AND FREQUENCY*

The union catalogue, to serve its purpose as a location tool, must be kept constantly up-to-date, with special attention paid to the inclusion of new titles and to scientific and technical literature. A regular arrangement is needed to provide complete and accurate inventories reflecting new, changed and deleted records. Both bibliographic and holdings data are susceptible to frequent change, not only because the elements are volatile, but also because reprints and microform editions may become available. Frequent new editions are also important in the case of deteriorating materials such as newspapers, where holdings statements do not remain stable for long periods of time. The only category in which up-to-dateness may be of lesser importance is historical bibliographies (see 9.5).

Frequency of printed issues will depend upon the size of the union catalogue, and the professional, technical and financial resources available to prepare the records and edit the input. The Project Director should make provision for new editions at frequent intervals and endeavour to minimize the gap between data collection and publication. The date of the contributions in respect of holdings is more significant than the date of publication of the union catalogue.

Each print or microfiche edition should be complete in itself. Supplements should be avoided, wherever possible, because they represent multiple sequences for the user to check.

If manual methods have to be used, techniques should be avoided which add to the difficulty of up-dating, such as numbering the entries, or using numbers within entries and indexes, which have to be re-sequenced in the next edition. Likewise, the use of multiple type-fonts, and complicated spacing and punctuation, increases the work of proof-reading and maintaining accuracy.

The normal objective should be a complete new edition once a year. All machine-readable systems facilitate systematic up-dating. Use of microfiche enables new editions to be produced at more frequent intervals. On-line systems offer the most efficient method of up-dating data and making it rapidly available.

Chapter 4

Scope

4   Several decisions regarding scope need to be made at the outset. These include the following:-

(a) The definition of a serial and of a newspaper.
(b) The area of coverage represented by the contributing institutions: single library system; group of independent libraries on a local, regional, national or international basis; and the relationships between these levels.
(c) The comprehensiveness of coverage in respect of types of serials, formats, languages, subjects, imprints, etc.

These decisions should be made in the light of the general convenience of the target audience and not of narrow specialist interests.

The choice of actual titles to be included should be left to the judgment of professional librarians. Once the scope has been determined, editors should strive for consistency in criteria for inclusion from one edition to the next, and avoid frequent exceptions.

While a balance must always be maintained in the desirable, the feasible and the economically possible, selectivity should not result from inadequate funds, size limitations, or data processing considerations such as insufficient space. But selectivity should be exercised in omitting titles reported which are outside the scope of the project. Inclusion of irrelevant material and problems with general, interdisciplinary and "grey" areas, can be avoided by making the scope as comprehensive as possible or limiting it to a narrow subject field.

4.1   *DEFINITIONS*

The definition of a *serial* should be uniform for all union catalogues and internationally accepted. The one recommended is that of the International Serials Data System (see 1.1.1 and *Appendix I*).

The definition of a *newspaper* for union catalogues of newspapers is considered in Chapter 9 (see 9.1).

4.2   AREA OF COVERAGE

Increased interlending in an era of financial stringency, and increased user expectations resulting from technological developments, reinforce the need to standardize guidelines which define the roles and interrelationships of types or levels of libraries for resource-sharing within each country. Such standardization is outside the concerns of the present *Guidelines,* but levels of sharing responsibility can to some extent be matched by levels of contribution to an hierarchical structure of union catalogue activities from local through regional to national, and the defining of self-sufficiency at which each should aim. These levels may relate to co-ordinated protocol areas facilitating cooperation and help to create a national location and information *network* for serial publications, while encouraging the user to observe protocols, exhaust local resources first, and assist in solving the problem of achieving a better balance between net lenders and net borrowers. An hierarchical lending system, undergirded by effective union catalogues of serials, may be more appropriate for large geographical areas with distributed library resources than a national serials lending centre.

The high cost of communications may result in future in regionalization of networking activities from a national bibliographic data base and the linking of nationwide consortia. Distribution of data between a national and a regional file can be an automatic operation, if desired, and a national union catalogue segmented into jurisdictional or regional editions or produced for specific groups such as academic libraries.

4.2.1   ROLE OF THE NATIONAL BIBLIOGRAPHIC AGENCY

Since national bibliographic agencies are responsible for preparing authoritative and comprehensive bibliographic records for serials of the national imprint, often maintain the national centre for the registration of serials in the International Serials Data System, act as the national centre for the international exchange of records, and serve as the international lending information centre, such institutions are particularly suited to construct and maintain the national union catalogue of serials, and co-ordinate the interface with international network nodes. This in turn ensures that the records so produced follow international cataloguing principles, use international bibliographic standards and codes such as the ISSN, and benefit from an authority file to control national corporate body and geographic names and uniform titles, in accordance with internationally-agreed guidelines, thus furthering the objectives of the UBC concept and programme adopted by UNESCO and IFLA. It is also advisable that the national bibliographic agency rationalize and co-ordinate the development of union catalogues throughout the country, including the linking of regional centres to the national location service, and the synchronization of authority/bibliographic files.

Such a network of libraries, with the national bibliographic agency as the core, enables all serial publications existing in a given territory to be made available, while the only serials required from abroad should be those not found in a domestic library.

4.3 NATURE OF COLLECTIONS TO BE INCLUDED

In addition to helping to define interrelations between types and levels of libraries, it is also possible to specify through such an hierarchy the nature of the collections which it is particularly important to make known from local through regional to national. The degree of specificity in reporting will vary from shelf location in the local institution to selected institutions at the national level.

The range of area of contribution will vary with the size of the country. A proliferation of small union catalogues produced by different methods, of varying completeness and reliability, is undesirable in a small nation. In a larger one, such a variety of sources to consult may be unavoidable, and even useful within an hierarchical structure as indicated above.

While the range may differ, eliminating conflict within the range can reduce duplication and facilitate exchange of data.

4.3.1 SINGLE LIBRARY SYSTEM

The union catalogue of a large system operating under a single jurisdiction, with several major collections in the same locality, or spread over one or more cities, should include all titles and all copies in all branches. It should facilitate reader access to the total resources of the university library or other complex. It should also include titles on order and in process to avoid unnecessary duplication of collections in branches of a system which are administratively connected.

Such institutional union catalogues usually include more specific information on locations, services and availability, than those for other areas of contribution.

4.3.2 LOCAL

Local union catalogues should aim for maximum comprehensiveness, including all titles published and all titles held in the locality. It is desirable that all copies should be covered, but participating institutions should also arrange to flag one copy for reporting from the local to the regional catalogue.

Material listed in local systems seldom appears in the national unless it is rare, and small libraries are often omitted from larger union catalogues. Thus the possibility exists to make known the resources of small school, public and special libraries, data concerning which would congest national catalogues. Together with the holdings of larger institutions, such information enables the user to determine if his needs to borrow or consult material can be met in his own locality.

Local union catalogues have greater value for co-operative acquisition, rationalization of collections, and integration of files, than those of larger area of coverage. They are of particular bibliographic importance when efforts have been made to ensure the inclusion of locally-published historical, archival, municipal, newspaper and ethnic serials, to reflect the wealth of local repositories, and to show the preservation status in the area, as such material is not always included in the national bibliography. It may be useful to include data concerning proposed acquisitions, titles on order and in process, proposed cancellations, and surplus materials available for disposal.

4.3.3 REGIONAL

Regional union catalogues may be defined on varying scales of geographic proximity. They complement national versions which restrict the number of locations displayed and in cases where there are many important institutions in the area. The value depends on the number and richness of the libraries grouped together, and the extent to which the user can determine if he can visit the institution himself or obtain material rapidly through proximity to a holding institution. They are essential building-blocks in any national information system, but may be ends in themselves.

In countries with a multitude of vernaculars, several regional union catalogues may be preferable to, and replace, a national union catalogue of serials. In countries without a central lending library, several regional union catalogues of serials may constitute a decentralized co-operative system.

The regional catalogue should aim to include all of the libraries in the area, and, in the case of multiple copies, one copy of each title held in each institution as designated by the reporting library.

Catalogues of this nature are particularly powerful tools if they reflect some form of network or pattern of co-operation in acquisition and resource-sharing, and if they are products of data bases which can draw standard records from, and coordinate with, a national union catalogue.

If the region equates with a jurisdiction (state, province, county, etc.), the union catalogue is of particular bibliographic importance when efforts have been made to ensure the inclusion of the jurisdiction's government document serials, historical association publications, etc., to reflect the wealth of state and other repositories, and show the preservation status in the area.

It may be useful to include data concerning proposed acquisitions, titles on order and in process, proposed cancellations, and surplus materials available for disposal.

4.3.4   *NATIONAL*

National union catalogues of serials should reflect resources in domestic serials and include all the domestic holdings of the national bibliographic agency (or all major libraries if bibliographic resources are not concentrated in one major depository library), and provide as comprehensive a selection as possible of similar imprints held throughout the country, and show the preservation status. Details of older domestic publications which precede the establishment of the national bibliography are extremely important. Inclusion of the foreign serials held by the national library, and a selection of the most important foreign titles held throughout the country, help to prevent unnecessary demands on the resources of other nations.

It is of prime importance that national union catalogues of serials indicate as fully as possible the holdings of former territories which are now independent, to identify the national serials literature dispersed in various institutions and private collections, and show the extent of its preservation.

National union catalogues should also show that universally useful serials, particularly the more important research materials, are available throughout the country at strategic points, while making specialist, unique and rare serial holdings more widely known.

4.3.5 INTERNATIONAL

Union catalogues of serials which reach beyond national boundaries vary considerably, from those of contiguous countries or states forming a natural geographic region, to those compiled on a world-wide basis to show the state of preservation of highly-specialized and rare titles. Such international co-operative schemes contribute to Universal Availability of Publications by providing a method of access to serial holdings in the libraries of other countries, and to universal inventory and preservation of early and other rarely-held serial materials.

4.4 COMPREHENSIVENESS

This should be the aim of all union catalogues of serials except those devoted to a narrow subject field. It is a factor which will vary depending on the area of coverage, but, in general, the most valuable union catalogues from local to national are those which have *no limitations*, i.e. they cover:-

— all types of serials;
— current and retrospective serials;
— all periods;
— all languages;
— all scripts;
— all subjects;
— all serial publishers;
— all countries;
— all formats (original, reprint, microform);
— all media (print and non-print);
— all intellectual levels;
— all types of contributing libraries;

—the holdings of one copy of each title reported by all contributing libraries.

It is particularly important that retrospective serials be included, and failure to convert such data into machine-readable form can result in the creation of new union catalogues which are less useful than the manual systems they are attempting to replace.

Titles should not be omitted because of the lack of an ISSN. Rather, opportunity should be taken in compiling machine-readable union catalogues to request, from the appropriate centre, ISSNs for serials which have not yet been registered in the International Serials Data System (see 6.1.4).

Likewise, titles should not be omitted because of difficulty of cataloguing the material, e.g. government documents, or assumption on the part of the compiler that certain titles are ephemeral in nature, or of minor interest, or not available for interlending. Providing the titles fit into the general scope, all serials reported by contributors should automatically be included.

Special efforts should be made to show resources in serials published by developing countries. Such materials are often difficult to obtain on account of poor distribution facilities. Their inclusion also helps to inventory older publications of these countries preceding legal deposit or held only in the libraries of former colonial rulers.

Selective union catalogues may be produced by:-

—type of serial;
—current or retrospective serials;
—period;
—language;
—script;
—subject;
—type of publisher;
—domestic or foreign;
—place of publication;
—format;
—medium;
—intellectual level;
—type of contributing library;

but ideally these should be obtained as by-products on demand from a general, comprehensive union catalogue (see 11.2).

Each union catalogue should normally be self-sufficient, i.e. the entries should not refer the user to other sources of basic bibliographic data nor of earlier, later or more specific holdings information, nor of other types of serials. (It is recognized that, for certain categories, e.g. newspapers, incunabula, the scholar with highly-specialized interests may need to consult other types of bibliographies or publishing histories for rarely-used data concerning individual serials.)

Further comments on comprehensiveness are included in these *Guidelines* under the various types of union catalogues.

Appendix I lists the types of serials which should be reported to union catalogues to ensure uniformity of inclusion.

Chapter 5

Compilation

5.1 The *method of compilation* will vary according to the following factors:-

(a) Type of union catalogue (general; subject; newspaper; historical bibliography; etc.).
(b) Nature of compiler (individual; institution; library association; local, regional or national bibliographic agency; bibliographic utility; transmission of data by direct magnetic tape delivery or record transfer from one data base to another; replication of an existing union catalogue).
(c) Area of contribution (single institution; group of independent libraries on a local, regional, national or international basis).
(d) Resources available (funds; personnel; data bases; computer equipment and programmes).
(e) Display medium (print; microform; CRT terminal).

It should be determined by the Project Director and the editorial staff.

Bibliographic data should be derived only from reliable sources, such as the actual serial, or a surrogate supplied by a duly authorized library, or machine-readable data extracted from authoritative external bases such as national bibliographic agency cataloguing, MARC-Serials tapes, the CONSER (Conversion of Serials) Project, and the national and international files of the International Serials Data System.

The many variables involved preclude the formulation of a generalized compilation methodology. It is not possible within the confines of the present *Guidelines* to detail the many alternatives, but it is recommended that compilers make maximum use of machine-readable methods, techniques and files.

5.2 USE OF MACHINE-READABLE RECORDS

5.2.1 Machine-readable data, once created, can be reorganized or accessed in many ways, and serve many functions, provided the information required by each one has been captured and the necessary explicit analysis has been made in terms comprehensible to the computer.

The union catalogue of serials in machine-readable form offers new ways of recording information, new services for users, and new possibilities for international exchange. In some countries, national bibliographic agencies, consortia and individual institutions are already exchanging tapes and building-up large national and international serials data bases with holdings records included.

Development trends in telecommunications networks presage direct linkages among bibliographic data bases with use of standardized communications protocols (see 12.9).

Efforts are also being made to link up large serials data bases with information retrieval facilities, thus enabling the user to search for appropriate serial literature references, locate the issues specifically required, and generate his own inter-library-loan requests on-line. Document ordering systems are available in conjunction with some on-line union catalogues.

As national mechanization systems have been planned, the need for international *technical* standards in developing national equivalents has been recognized. Most of the national processing formats of the MARC family (such as LC/MARC) have as their basis the international standard record structure ISO 2709 (Format for Bibliographic Information Interchange on Magnetic Tape), as do the international exchange formats which have more recently been created, such as UNIMARC and those currently in use within the information community. A single format which would incorporate or integrate the requirements of the abstracting, indexing and library communities within one interchange standard is now being developed. Once this Common Communication Format is available, a greater range of serials services may be expected.

5.2.2 While machine-readable files offer the most opportunities to share records and reduce cataloguing costs, sharing can only be successful if *bibliographic* standards are agreed upon and scrupulously followed. Utilizing the MARC-Serials cataloguing and exchange formats successfully entails creating records which meet standards for content, quality and consistency of practice, while headings for corporate names (and also for subjects, if this approach is used) require a centrally-controlled authority file.

Some countries using national MARC-Serials formats (e.g. Canada) have developed union catalogue accession reporting versions, allowing flexibility in the fullness of data which is input, thus reducing coding costs while still retaining the MARC structure.[2]

5.2.3 To the standards for bibliographic control must be added those for *holdings* control, and constant attention to ensuring that these two, and equally important, components are adequately balanced and working in tandem. Some countries (e.g. Canada) have expanded the national MARC-Serials format to produce a standard for reporting and exchanging holdings information, to facilitate display in union catalogues, and to allow machine-reading of a location enquiry and automatic generation of an inter-library-loan request according to pre-defined geographic and other criteria.[3]

Without common agreement on both bibliographic and holdings standards, the ability of a union catalogue of serials to communicate to all kinds of users, and further the UBC and UAP programmes, will be seriously impaired.

5.2.4 *SOURCES OF MACHINE-READABLE DATA*

It may be possible to acquire machine-readable records from another organization, but unless such a data base has identical standards to that required, time-consuming editing and enhancing of the supplied records may offset expected savings in staff time and effort in creating the file.

Automated matching of a machine-readable file against an existing MARC data base to derive or replace records, or amalgamate them to create a union catalogue, depends for its success on developing an effective matching algorithm, plus some manual review. It is essential that all machine-readable serials files include the ISSN, thus enabling data to be transferred economically from local files to union catalogues, and ensuring the most vital serials element is provided for any programme to compare or amalgamate automated files for various purposes.

It is emphasized that merging multi-institutional machine-readable serials files is not a simple procedure. Technological developments which permit linkages among systems, data base loading of tapes into a system, and transfer of data from one to another, *without human review,* pose problems. Linking of, and exchange of information among, union serials files require not only co-ordination and strict adherence of each of the compilers to the same tagging, formatting, and cataloguing practices, but also due consideration as to whether (a) the bibliographic, and (b) the holdings, segments match.

Records created outside the national bibliographic agency should be translatable into a standard MARC-Serials format, in order that bibliographic data can be communicated to and extracted from national and international MARC files, thus realizing the benefits of shared data creation and furthering the development of serials networks and location systems.

Utilization of a large serials data base such as that of the CONSER Project, which contains over a quarter of a million current and retrospective titles, prevents costly duplication of record conversion in individual libraries and further proliferation of machine-readable files which are incompatible with one another and with any of the nationally or internationally accepted standards. This major achievement in co-operative activity has resulted from national and other large libraries and consortia, chosen on the basis of their excellence in serials cataloguing, using agreed-upon conventions and input standards. Such a large single source offers the possibility of building-up, enriching, upgrading or replacing records in existing machine-readable files in individual libraries and consortia, and the maximum flexibility to participate in co-operative programmes or convert to another facility.

5.2.5 SOURCES OF HOLDINGS DATA

Under no circumstances should holdings be obtained from second-hand sources. Compiling a union catalogue of serials necessitates the acquisition of this data directly from each contributor, and the frequent checking of its accuracy and currency.

Chapter 6

Bibliographic Control

6 Uniformity of cataloguing rules and practices is essential to organize serials information for retrieval in a union catalogue. Whether this is produced in print or microform, or made available in on-line display, the problem of integrating multiple bibliographic records into one consistent and unified catalogue has to be solved.

6.1 *CATALOGUING CODES AND STANDARDS*

6.1.1 Bibliographic records are prepared in accordance with cataloguing codes. There is no international code or compilation of cataloguing rules in existence. Three multi-national codes are used in a number of countries:-

Anglo-American cataloguing rules. 2d ed. 1978 (AACR2). Prepared by an editorial committee representing Canadian, United Kingdom and United States librarians.
Regeln für die alphabetische Katalogisierung (RAK). Prepared by and used in a number of German-language countries.
Uniform rules. Prepared by the USSR Cataloguing Committee and used throughout the USSR and some other Socialist countries.

These codes include stipulations for describing serials, determining the responsibility for authorship of serials issued by corporate bodies, and deciding on the form of the corporate name.

6.1.2 The *International Standard Bibliographic Description for Serials* (ISBD(S)), developed within IFLA as part of the UBC programme, provides a standard for the description and identification of printed serial publications, assigns an order to the elements of the description, and specifies a system of punctuation for that description. It has been incorporated in a number of national cataloguing codes as well as RAK and AACR2.

While primarily concerned with current publications, it does make some provision for recording serials which have ceased publication or changed their titles.

6.1.3 Since the union catalogue must integrate records from many countries, but is primarily intended for users within the country of publication, it is expected that bibliographic records will appear in the language(s) of the latter. If records are extracted from several national bibliographies, each using their own language(s), it may be helpful to the user to replace history notes connecting earlier and later titles with symbols.

6.1.4 Essential to the standardization of records is the *International Standard Serial Number* (ISSN). This is used in conjunction with the "key-title" of a serial. Key-titles and ISSNs are assigned by the National and Regional Centres of the International Serials Data System (ISDS), co-ordinated by the International Centre for the Registration of Serial Publications in Paris, and disseminated through the publications of these centres. ISDS is an inter-governmental organization established within the framework of the UNESCO UNISIST Programme, and aims to provide a reliable registry of world serial publications. The ISSN is an eight-digit code based on ISO standard 3297. This unique number facilitates identification in national and international sources, and can provide a link between bibliographic data bases, and between bibliographic and other data bases such as SDI services.

6.2 *AUTHORITY FILES*

It is advisable to establish an authority system for names and uniform titles, to ensure consistency in the union file. An *automated* authority system can control the structure of the bibliographic file, eliminate redundant data entry and storage, provide easy maintenance if a standard is changed, and make the information accessible to other organizations.

6.3 *MINIMUM DATA ELEMENTS FOR BIBLIOGRAPHIC CONTROL*

Standardization of union catalogues of serials requires that there be uniformity of information displayed in print, microform or on-line, regardless of the amount stored in data banks for other purposes. A "finding list" is inadequate to realize all the potential of this kind of bibliographic tool, but a display of entries to the level of fullness of ISBD(S) is not required, particularly for interlending purposes and for users on a known-item search. The effectiveness of all information sources is directly related to the ability of the users, and too much information can be as great a problem as too little. Clarity and simplicity of approach in serials cataloguing often serve the general user best.

6.3.1 It is therefore necessary to specify a set of key data elements. This is determined by the following factors:-

(1) The majority of users of serials catalogues are on a known-item search.[4]
(2) Bibliographic and holdings data are of equal importance, interrelated, and shed light on each other.
(3) Long strings of bibliographic information tend to obscure the most essential data and overwhelm the holdings data.
(4) All serials constitute material characterized by bibliographic instability. Their intrinsically mutable nature demands that descriptive cataloguing be reduced to the minimum to avoid costly recataloguing of inessential elements.
(5) A serials system which is inexpensive to maintain, update and use, offers the greatest potential for co-operation and resource-sharing.

6.3.2 Compilers of union catalogues of serials should therefore aim at a mid-point between a full bibliographic record and a finding list, to produce a tool which provides the following:-

(1) Authoritative, unique identification of each serial.
(2) Access by all titles and by all issuing bodies, regardless of the cataloguing rules followed.
(3) Access by significant information retrieval numbers.
(4) Linkage of segments for serials which have changed their title and/or issuing body.
(5) Clarification of the holdings data.
(6) Clarification of microforms and reprints held.

Such a tool consisting of a practical sub-set of essential bibliographic data elements, used in conjunction with an essential set of holdings data elements (see 7.4), should help to prevent the submission of "blind" and "speculative" interlending requests with their attendant uncertainties and costs. It should enable the general user to find a serial when he knows some element of identification, such as one of its titles or its sponsoring organizations, to review the titles issued by each such sponsor, and to look at a display of actual library holdings in meaningful collocation.

Such a union short record system should also facilitate the co-operative development and/or exchange of data and ensure compatibility through a common level of elements for communications purposes.

6.3.3　　In order to make certain that the functions noted in Chapter 2 can be satisfactorily performed, the following *minimum bibliographic data element set* is recommended for use in conjunction with the *minimum holdings data element set* discussed in Chapter 7:-

UNIFORM TITLE (see 6.4)
TITLE PROPER
GENERAL MATERIAL DESIGNATION (for non-print serials)
CORPORATE BODY (issuing, publishing or sponsoring the serial)
EDITION STATEMENT
NUMERIC/CHRONOLOGICAL DESIGNATION (given in the vernacular)
PLACE OF PUBLICATION (first)
NOTES:

1. Linking—relationship of the serial to its predecessor and successor.
2. Clarifying holdings—numbering and dating peculiarities, suspensions, etc.
3. Describing microform/reprint edition—variations from original.

ISSN = key-title
NATIONAL BIBLIOGRAPHY CONTROL AND RETRIEVAL NUMBER(S).

The variations applicable only to union catalogues of *newspapers* are discussed in 9.1.

Alternatives and options are not recommended, since a code for use by multiple libraries in a networking situation necessitates one practice only for consistency and standardized results.

6.3.3.1 Limitations of size, cost, or difficulty of procuring data, should not impede attainment of the above mandatory set of elements. It should be possible to generate this simple, standardized format from a cataloguing record created in accordance with such multi-national codes as AACR2. Ideally, such a sub-set should be a by-product of the national bibliographic record, thus ensuring reliability for all national imprints. Similarly foreign imprints should preferably be extracted from the records of the national bibliographic agencies concerned.

6.3.3.2 In a single-entry bibliography, it is axiomatic that serials entered under title will also be provided with access by the corporate body or bodies associated with them, and serials entered under corporate body or bodies will also be provided with access by title proper.

Additional access points should be provided for earlier, later, and other varying forms of names of corporate bodies. Similarly access should be given by all variant and parallel titles, initialisms, abbreviations, acronyms, etc.

In computerized systems, the necessary data should be collected and coded to provide flexibility of choice in filing elements, so that output can be produced which satisfies the requirements of both title and corporate-author cataloguing, while enabling essential indexes (such as ISSN) and other appropriate sequences (e.g. geographic) to be supplied.

6.3.3.3 In cases where successful location may require recourse to fuller bibliographic information, the need can be met by standard reference sources, such as national bibliographies, or, in the case of on-line systems, by providing the option of a full bibliographic entry from which the "mini" record was extracted as well as the mini record itself.

6.4 *UNIFORM TITLE, TITLE PROPER AND KEY-TITLE*

6.4.1 Uniform titles are needed for *title identification, file organization,* and *linking connected items.*

6.4.2 When the title proper is identical to the title proper of another serial in the same catalogue or data base, it is necessary to resolve the conflict by creating a uniform title consisting of the title proper and a parenthetical qualifier such as corporate body, place, date, edition, etc. This uniform title concept provides a means of distinguishing among serials entered under title which have the same title proper or among serials entered under the name of a corporate body which have the same combination of name heading and title proper. In such instances, both the uniform title and the title proper should be displayed, in that order.

6.4.3 When such uniform titles exist, they should also be used as the filing title and in linkages. In all other cases, the title proper should be used for these purposes.

6.4.4 Such uniform serial titles will sometimes coincide with the key-title created in accordance with the *Guidelines for ISDS*.[5]

6.5 *CHANGES OF TITLE OR CORPORATE RESPONSIBILITY*

Since serials frequently change their titles and/or issuing bodies, a consistent policy is also needed to handle this problem. It is essential to define the bibliographic entity, which, in turn, dictates when a new record is or is not necessary.

6.5.1 The principle of *successive-entry cataloguing* should be adopted for the following reasons:-

(1) Correlation with the title as cited for the user on a known-item search, which title should coincide with the identification on the serial at time of original publication (or, in the case of corporate bodies, with the name in the reference and on the publication).
(2) Correlation between entries in bibliographic tools and library-generated tools.
(3) Speed of access to serial literature.
(4) Avoidance of duplication of records and scattering of holdings if a mixture of policies is followed in the same union catalogue.

6.5.1.1 It is nonetheless recognized that it may sometimes be necessary to catalogue under the earliest, latest, best-known or longest-lived title, if insufficient information is available to describe the various segments, and that some changes of very short duration or very minor character may not justify the creation of a new bibliographic record. Newspapers (see 9.1) are often difficult to catalogue according to the successive-entry principle.

6.5.2 Adherence to this principle results in the following rules:-

(1) If the title proper of a serial changes, a separate bibliographic record should be made for each title.
(2) If the name of a corporate body under which a serial is entered changes, a separate bibliographic record should be made for each name of the corporate body.
(3) If a serial is entered under a corporate body responsible for it, and there is a change in responsibility, a separate bibliographic record should be made for each of the bodies responsible.

6.5.3 The use of successive-entry cataloguing entails editing all contributed holdings to correspond with each discrete bibliographic unit (see 7.3).

6.5.4 Display of history and holdings under latest title or earliest title, as well as successive, through machine linkages of segments and special programming, provides a capability which is most valuable for librarians wishing to find the entire bibliographic history of a serial in one place. It results in repetition of entries in printed and fiche editions, but should be considered a standard display feature in on-line systems which do not have the same space constraints.

6.6 *MICROFORMS AND OTHER REPRODUCED MATERIAL*

Much of the output of reprint firms consists of serials, while microfilming projects, particularly to preserve materials, frequently result in duplicate filming of the same title, though not necessarily with uniformity of content. Microfilming of newspapers, above all, produces many variants of what is often (erroneously) assumed to be the "same" text as the "original", when the original has bibliographically varying editions, the editions filmed and issues located for filming differ, and it is further necessary to differentiate types of microform, to indicate polarity, and to distinguish between master, preservation master, and service microforms.

6.6.1 Serials in reproduction have not yet received adequate attention in the area of descriptive cataloguing, and the needs of serials management systems and union catalogues of serials which utilize the bibliographic records created according to national and international standards have not yet been fully explored and accommodated.

6.6.1.1 Microforms are sometimes described in their own right and sometimes by means of a note added to the data concerning the original publication. For purposes of union catalogues of serials, and for serials management systems (for the two are closely inter-related), as well as facilitating preservation filming activities and giving scholarly access to bibliographic information, it is essential that original editions and microform editions (and variants within each category) be treated as *separate* bibliographic entities to which the relevant holdings statements can be appended.

Microform serials should be differentiated in respect of the following for *each* variant edition:-

—Type of microform.
—Place of micropublication.
—Micropublisher.
—Variations from the original edition (by means of Notes).

6.6.1.2 Likewise, reprints may exactly duplicate a previously published serial, or provide additional material, resulting in variant editions.

If the reprint exactly duplicates the original, there may be little point in creating a separate bibliographic record in a union catalogue, particularly given that institutions frequently purchase isolated volumes to fill in gaps and these volumes are merely substitutes for the original.

It is advisable that an edition of a previously published serial *not* an exact duplicate be given a separate bibliographic record, which identifies the reprint publisher, the place of publication, and provides notes regarding the variations from the original.

6.6.2 In machine systems, linkages should be provided between the record for the original format and that of any reproduction.

6.7 *NON-ROMAN SCRIPTS*

Most union catalogues of serials include titles in many languages, and it is often necessary to input serials in more than one script. Romanization is therefore an essential bibliographic tool and permits one sequence in one script. Many local and national romanization schemes exist, and there is no single internationally-accepted standard. The ISDS system in Paris is working on the standardization of romanization of serial titles.

An ISO or nationally accepted conversion scheme should be used. A note of the system should be given in the Introduction, specifying any local modifications or exceptions, and a key should be provided.

Since romanization is not a reliable control tool for the unambiguous identification of serials, nor a tool of bibliographic exchange, it is recommended that parallel bibliographic data in the vernacular script be provided as well as the romanized entry, and links be made between the romanized and original entries. In addition, the titles of serials in non-Roman scripts should be translated into the language predominant among the users of the union catalogue of serials, and the original language of the serial indicated in a note. References should be made from all translated titles, whether a parallel title appearing on the publication or the title as translated by the cataloguing agency.

Entries in the original script should be obtained through an appropriate service of the national bibliographic agency involved.

Entries in all scripts should conform to the general principles for union catalogues of serials outlined in these *Guidelines.*

It is recognized that until technological developments permit simultaneous display of texts in Roman and non-Roman alphabets, on-line union catalogues of serials will be unable to present data in the original non-Roman scripts.

Chapter 7

Holdings Control

7 Holdings statements in union catalogues of serials are of equal importance with bibliographic information, and require the same attention to accessibility, currency, consistency and quality. To support all functions, it is essential that bibliographic and location control be integrated.

7.1 Effective creation and utilization of holdings statements is dependent on two factors:-

(1) the assignment of *adequate personnel* in each participating institution to collect input and keep it constantly up-to-date, and in the union catalogue office to co-ordinate and maintain all input to the required standard;

(2) the use of a *standard* covering the data areas, elements, and levels of detail within, for reporting and display.

7.2 The many problems in expressing the complexities of holdings in numerical and/or chronological sequences or in retention statements, and the need for universality of understanding of such data, require that all participants report holdings to the same standard.

There is at present no international standard for reporting holdings, nor any international standard for exchanging holdings data in machine-readable form. Some countries (e.g. Canada) have expanded the MARC-Serials Format to enable individual libraries to report to the national union catalogue by this method.[6] Location reporting as a by-product of a library's local serials control system may be accomplished by magnetic tape or on-line transmission. Such communication entails following the prescribed standard, and also the capability to select reportable records, including new, changed or deleted since the last report, to keep track of records which have already been reported, and to use history and treatment codes to up-date local files and reflect the generation of an accession report. It may be possible, in the case of some types of serials, to derive summarized holdings statements automatically from the detailed holdings data required by individual libraries.

Though both manual and machine-readable national standards exist, they are still in a limited stage of development, and do not yet encompass all types of serials, nor all the complexities and inconsistencies within these types.

Until an international standard is available, adherence to the general principles, and use of the data elements, outlined below are recommended to provide a minimum reporting standard. It is suitable for both manual and mechanized systems. In conjunction with the minimum bibliographic data element set (see 6.3.3), which includes data needed to clarify holdings statements (numeric/chronological designations of the serial, edition statement, notes on suspensions and numbering peculiarities and describing microform and reprint variations), it should help to ensure a successful outcome to librarian and patron use of such statements.

These guidelines for holdings statements are independent of any cataloguing system.

7.3   GENERAL PRINCIPLES

All holdings reported, whether for print, fiche or on-line catalogues, require editorial control to guarantee uniformity in presentation and adherence to standards.

Holdings statements should be gathered together under one form of the title, and reflect only that portion of a serial title represented by one bibliographic description to which they are linked (see 6.5).

Holdings should be positive in nature, expressing what is held by means of numerical and/or chronological designations.

Holdings should be expressed in *summarized condensed form,* indicating gaps and incomplete volumes or years (see 7.7 Example Statements). This level of specificity should be consistently maintained to avoid "speculative" approaches on inter-library-loan and to meet the needs of the maximum number of librarians and patrons.

Separate bibliographic editions should have separate bibliographic records and separate holdings statements should be provided for originals, microforms and some reprints (see 6.6.1).

Arbitrary numbering and/or dating systems assigned by publishers to hard-copy and microform reprints should be disregarded.

Open entries should be used only to indicate that the holdings are complete from the volume and/or year specified.

Institutional symbols should be used only to indicate ownership and location.

The number of copies to be reported should vary according to the area of contribution, ranging from all copies for a local file to one copy (the most complete and/or most available) per institutional symbol for national reporting.

Each statement should reflect an actual file, i.e. composite statements consolidating data for several copies into one statement should not be used.

Serials which are constantly cumulating their contents should be reported in terms of major cumulations.

Translation journals should be reported in terms of the numerical and/or chronological designations of the translation journal, not the original language numbers and dates, if both systems are utilized on the translation.

Only information of universal interest should be reported.

7.4 MINIMUM DATA ELEMENTS FOR HOLDINGS CONTROL

Data is required of three different types:-

(1) Institutions which possess the serial, and their locations.
(2) Range of holdings of each institution, in terms of the enumeration and/or chronology system used by the publishers, or retention statements.
(3) Notes which clarify the holdings of each institution.

Data should be presented in that order and displayed in columns which are easy to scan and interpret.

7.4.1 INSTITUTION IDENTIFICATION AND LOCATION

The names of contributing institutions are normally represented by alpha or alphanumeric symbols. Although this locator is a key data element common to much of the information exchange within the bibliographic community, there is at present no international standard which uniquely identifies institutions and collections. Pending the issuance of such a standard, it is recommended that all union catalogues of serials produced within a country use the nationally-recognized system. National bibliographic agencies are frequently the centres for assigning symbols to requesting institutions, maintaining the register of symbols and addresses, and publishing directories containing this information, for national union catalogue reporting purposes.

It is advisable that the symbol used be meaningful, mnemonic, contain elements of geographic location and type of library, and be amenable to computer manipulation. Each symbol should be concise, unique and unambiguous for each library and collection represented in the union catalogue.

In displaying symbols plus holdings and other related data, records should be grouped together geographically, so that the user can determine the most convenient location if he wishes to consult the material, and interlending services can obtain material rapidly through knowledge of the nearest source of supply.

Full details of the institution or collection to which the symbol applies should be included in the Introduction (see 8.1.1).

At the local and institutional level, the location information may need to be more specific.

For some purposes (e.g. union catalogues of newspapers), it is sometimes useful to include the holdings of publishers and private individuals.

7.4.2 RANGE OF HOLDINGS OF EACH INSTITUTION

The majority of serials bear both numerical and chronological designations by which they can be arranged, recorded and cited. Some, e.g. annual reports, may bear only chronological designations. Others, e.g. newspapers, are normally cited by date even though they may also carry numerical descriptions.

Multiple numbering or multiple dating systems on the same serial frequently occur. Some terms and systems are unique to one publication. Reprinters may assign additional (and arbitrary) designations. Legislative serial documents are normally described and cited by the number of the legislature, session and date, as well as by other numerical sequences. Any confusion or inconsistency on the publisher's part further complicates the problems of expressing holdings meaningfully.

With the major exception of newspapers, holdings of those

serials which bear numerical designations should normally be described in these terms, since this allows the greatest level of precision. The full extent of the file, indicating any incomplete volumes, should be described in this sequence, since it is not always possible to indicate which dates are incomplete. Inclusive dates should be added as a further help to the user who has only a date citation.

7.4.2.1 ENUMERATION DATA

Enumeration data does not require the prefixing of captions (such as series, volume, number, etc.) if the numeric/chronological designations have been described in the bibliographic area (see 6.3.3), except in the following circumstances:-

(1) to clarify which enumeration system is being used when multiple possibilities occur in the same serial;
(2) to clarify incomplete holdings when the serial changes its enumeration system;
(3) to clarify incomplete holdings when a succession of series is involved.

Such designation captions, when used, should be given in an abbreviated form in the *vernacular,* corresponding to the description in the bibliographic area. There is at present no international table of abbreviations which covers all types of enumeration systems in use in all languages.

If the serial bears more than one numbering system, only one should be used in the holdings statement. The one chosen should be clarified by prefixing an abbreviated caption in the vernacular, as indicated above.

Specific holdings should be expressed, indicating any gaps or incompleteness by means of the standard symbols (see 7.6).

All enumeration data should be reported as Arabic numerals.

All ordinal numbers should be converted into cardinal numbers.

7.4.2.2 CHRONOLOGY DATA

If the holdings are being described in numerical terms, a *beginning date* only is required for a currently acquired serial, and *inclusive dates* for a dead serial or one which is not currently being acquired.

If the serial uses only a chronological system, or this is the primary reporting feature (as in the case of newspapers), specific holdings should be expressed in these terms, indicating any gaps or incompleteness by means of the standard symbols (see 7.6).

Overlapping years and calendar years should be differentiated (see 7.6 Punctuation Conventions and Abbreviations, and 7.7 Example Statements).

Dates used to express holdings should be those which will be found in citations, i.e. nominal, or coverage, or edition, or date of meeting, etc. Publication dates may be used if none of these categories is present. When several types of chronological systems are given on the same serial, that used in citations should take preference.

The following types of dates should *not* be used, as they normally have no meaning in the context of serial citation:-

- —manufacture
- —printing
- —reprinting
- —release
- —distribution
- —copyright
- —volume title-page variants printed after year-end of issues.

If the serial uses more than one *significant* dating system, it may be necessary to report and display two sequences of chronology, e.g. Old and New Style English calendar, Christian and Hebrew calendar, Gregorian and French Republican calendar. The second sequence should be added in parentheses.

With the exception of newspapers, only the year is required.

Newspaper holdings should be described only in terms of the chronological sequence, and it may be necessary to include days, months, seasons, etc. which should be expressed in the vernacular.

It may also be necessary to use only the chronology in the following two situations:

(1) There has been so much confusion and inconsistency in the publisher's numbering system that a chronological expression is more meaningful.
(2) The publishers themselves have fluctuated in system used, resulting in a mixture of numerical and chronological sequences.

All chronology data should be reported in Arabic numerals. If the publication does not carry a date, none is supplied.

7.4.2.3 RETENTION DATA

Retention statements should be used in cases where the institution does not retain the file permanently. This is the only area in which *general* statements are acceptable. They are normally made in natural language, and describe the following two situations:-

(1) Serials received which the library discards on receipt.
(2) Serials received which the library retains for a period of time and then discards.

Statements may be specific or non-specific, e.g.

Non-specific	CURRENT ISSUES ONLY RETAINED
	LATEST EDITION ONLY RETAINED
	RETAINED UNTIL MICROFORM EDITION RECEIVED
Specific	NOT RETAINED
	CURRENT × NOS. ONLY RETAINED
	CURRENT × MONTHS ONLY RETAINED
	LAST × YEARS ONLY RETAINED
	LAST × EDITIONS ONLY RETAINED

[× = exact number of units or time-span, to be supplied by reporting library]

Abbreviations are not recommended for international use. It is suggested that the above commonly-used phrases and their equivalents in other languages be adopted as the norm.

7.4.3 NOTES CLARIFYING HOLDINGS

It is sometimes essential to include notes which clarify holdings, e.g. that the institution holds only the Sunday edition of a newspaper, or that the microform held is a library edition rather than a record edition. Such notes should be restricted to information of universal interest and be presented as concisely as possible.

The polarity (negative, positive, or both) is required for all microform holdings.

7.4.4 LOCAL CONTROL NUMBER

A local control number is required in machine-readable files as an access point to the local system, for up-dating holdings statements, and to assist in the generation of automated inter-library-loan requests.

7.4.5 DATE OF REPORT

This is essential in machine-readable files, both for original notification and subsequent amendments, and may also be useful in manual systems.

7.5 SUMMARY OF DATA ELEMENTS FOR REPORTING AND DISPLAY OF HOLDINGS

The following are the essential minimum data elements for *reporting* holdings and *displaying* them in print, microfiche and on-line union catalogues of serials:-

    INSTITUTION SYMBOL

        and

    RETENTION STATEMENT

        or

    VOLUMES/ISSUES HELD and *INCLUSIVE DATES*

        or

    DATES HELD

        and

    NOTES: (1) MICROFORM POLARITY
                (2) CLARIFICATION OF EDITION HELD

The following may also be essential to a particular system:-

    LOCAL SYSTEM CONTROL NUMBER

    DATE OF REPORT

7.6 PUNCTUATION CONVENTIONS AND ABBREVIATIONS

Symbol	Name	Purpose
-	hyphen	To indicate an *unbroken* range of holdings: (a) from the volume/issue or date specified to the present if the serial is currently being acquired; (b) between the volumes/issues or dates specified if the serial is dead or is not being currently acquired.
,	comma	To show a gap in a range of holdings.
;	semi-colon	To indicate a non-gap break (e.g. to show discontinuity in the publisher's enumeration/chronology).
[ ]	brackets	To indicate that the volumes or years so enclosed are not complete.
( )	parentheses	To indicate a *significant* alternate chronology.
?	question mark	To indicate uncertainty.
/	diagonal	A connector between notations that form a single published physical unit, e.g. a date which covers a single non-calendar year (1967/68) or a combined numbering (28/29).
n	microform polarity	To indicate microform held is negative.
p	microform polarity	To indicate microform held is positive.
n & p	microform polarity	To indicate both positive and negative microform are held.

Double punctuation should be avoided.

7.7 EXAMPLE STATEMENTS

The examples given below are illustrative only.

Example no.	Library Symbols	Holdings Statements
1)	CaBViV	1- 1968-
	CaOTU	CURRENT ISSUES ONLY RETAINED
2)	CaBViV	[1963,1965]-[1968]-
	CaOTU	1888-[1910]-

Example no.	Library Symbols	Holdings Statements	
3)	CaBViV	5723 (1962/63)-	
	CaOTU	5725 (1964/65)-5726 (1965/66), 5730 (1969/70)	
4)	CaBViV	1980- Sunday ed.	
	CaBViP	RETAINED UNTIL MICROFORM EDITION RECEIVED	
5)	CaBViV	1946- p	Library ed.
	CaBViP	1888- n&p	Record ed.
6)	CaBViV	[NSV.6-8]10[S3V.3-6,9]10,12[14,17-18]-47, 49-51	1910-72
	CaOTU	1-S3V.51	1820-72
7)	CaBViV	1949-51; V.8-	1949-
	CaOTU	1950-[V.8]-[14-15]-	1950-
8)	CaBViV	4-	1921-
	CaOTU	NSNO.13/14	1968
9)	CaBViV	3?,5-	1946-
	CaOTU	2?-	1945-
10)	CaBViV	NSV.22-24	1967-69
	CaOTU	1-	1931-
11)	CaBViV	P1-P2;V.1-	1969-
	CaOON	NOT RETAINED	
12)	CaBViV	1968-1,1968-4—	
	CaOONL	1967-2,1968-7	
13)	CaBViV	1969/70-1973/74,1977/78-	
	CaOON	1899/1900-	
14)	CaBViV	V.1A-NSNO.50	1936-53
	CaOON	V.4A-8A,10A;NSNO.1-	1936-

Chapter 8

Recommended Standards for Style, Presentation and Arrangement

8   In taking account of the universal use of union catalogues of serials, and the many types of agencies which compile them, it is apparent that there are great advantages in establishing some international uniformity not only in the contents but in the physical and editorial lay-out of printed and microfiche editions, and display in on-line systems.

8.1   The following recommendations are made with regard to the appearance and arrangement of *printed* editions, irrespective of method of production:-

—An international paper size (preferably A4) should be used.
—The lay-out and typography of the cover and title-page should be clear and unambiguous, and should include the following:-

(a) The title of the union catalogue. (This should be distinctive and adequately reflect the scope, by describing briefly the type, contributors, area, and period, if appropriate.)
(b) The edition designation.
(c) The place of publication.
(d) The name of the publisher.
(e) The date of publication.
(f) The ISSN (on the top right-hand corner of the front cover and on the title-page).

—The verso of the title-page should include the following:-

(a) Copyright information.
(b) Details of availability and price.
(c) Details of editing.

—An introduction should be provided (see 8.1.1).

—The main body of the text should be alphabetical by title (see 8.1.3).
—Indexes should be provided (see 8.1.4).

8.1.1 INTRODUCTION

Each edition should contain introductory material to help the various kinds of users. The Introduction should be complete in itself, and not require consultation of similar material in previous editions. All information should be up-dated as and when necessary.

In order to clarify the contents of the union catalogue and assist the user, this Introduction should outline the editorial policy and explain the following:-

(1) The objectives, potential audience, and expected functions.
(2) The scope: inclusions, exclusions.
(3) The frequency.
(4) The arrangement.
(5) The filing system, with examples (see 8.1.2).
(6) The cataloguing practices, with examples (see Chapter 6), including:-

—standards: choice of entry; form of entry; title abbreviations;
—policy on changes in titles and/or corporate responsibility;
—romanization schemes, including local modifications or exceptions, and display of the romanization tables;
—subject system, if used, with outline;
—indexes and other access features.

(7) The special terminology and abbreviations used.
(8) The holdings system (see Chapter 7).
(9) The symbols of contributing institutions, with full names, addresses, telephone and Telex numbers attached, and an alphabetical listing of the names of all contributors with the symbols attached (see 7.4.1).
(10) A statement on services and products available from the central machine-readable serials data base.

It may be possible under (9) to include the loan and photocopying policies of each institution, or other indication of availability. Such information should be obtained directly from the contributing libraries, and, once included, should be kept up-to-date. The highly specific and fluid nature of such data will often make it unavailable for inclusion, even in on-line services.

It is particularly helpful if the Introduction includes one or more complete sample entries with each element in the entry explained.

It is also helpful if this Introduction is repeated in each volume for editions of union catalogues which consist of more than one physical volume. Where appropriate, e.g. a country with more than one official language, the Introduction should be repeated in its entirety in all necessary languages.

8.1.2 FILING SYSTEM

In order to use the union catalogue successfully, the filing arrangement must be understood. As yet, there is no international agreement on standard filing practices nor on the romanization of non-Roman scripts. Problems will present themselves in both manual and computer-aided union catalogues, and will be complicated by the multiplicity of languages, and sometimes of scripts, to be integrated in the minimum number of sequences.

Because of current differences in practices, it is considered useful to include in each sequence the maximum of possible cross-references as an aid to the user. Transposition of words, or the omission of words, to effect specific filing arrangements, should be avoided.

A simple system, consistently maintained, should be adopted to sequence entries in an order comprehensible to the user. The practices followed should be explained in the Introduction and examples provided. Use of spacing, capitalization and underscoring, etc., may also help the user to follow the arrangement.

It is sometimes possible to interfile Roman and non-Roman scripts. Where such an arrangement cannot be effected, non-Roman scripts should be listed after all Roman script entries, or before them if the non-Roman script is the national one. In all cases, suitable cross-references should be made from one section to others.

8.1.3 ARRANGEMENT

The arrangement of the union catalogue should facilitate rapid access and efficient use. With the exception of catalogues devoted wholly to newspapers or government publications, the preferred print or display arrangement for the main sequence is *alphabetical by title.* This achieves the closest possible correspondence with bibliographic identifications in indexing and abstracting services, footnote citations in research papers and other scholarly works, well-known abbreviations for serials and recommended standards for abbreviating titles.

All entries for all languages should be integrated in the alphabetical sequence. It is nonetheless recognized that, except in cases where computer-controlled typesetting can merge Roman and non-Roman script records for display, separate sequences will have to be provided for each non-Roman script, with suitable cross-references linking the sections to the primary arrangement.

In all cases, other essential access points, such as issuing body, should be provided by means of indexes, references or other added entries, with the aim of giving multiple approaches appropriate to the type of union catalogue of serials covered, and to aid the user with an imprecise title citation.

In the case of union catalogues devoted wholly to newspapers, the preferred arrangement is *geographical,* with additional access by title (see 9.1).

In the case of union catalogues devoted wholly to government publications, the preferred arrangement is by *jurisdiction* (see 9.2).

8.1.4 *INDEXES*

Indexes may complement the arrangement of the main sequence and supply additional user information. Since the primary arrangement will normally be alphabetical by title, it is particularly helpful to add the following indexes:-

(a) A *corporate body index,* including all corporate names associated with each serial contained in the union catalogue, and preferably gathering together under each name brief details of each title issued, published or sponsored by that body.

(b) An *ISSN index* with related "key-titles" (see 6.1.4).

8.1.5 *REGISTER-INDEX FORMAT*

A register-index format with a master register of bibliographic records in random order by register number, plus continuously cumulating indexes by title, corporate responsibility, ISSN, and possibly subject, with brief descriptive data in one or more of the indexes, may result in publishing savings and offers multiple access points. But it does necessitate a double look-up for reference and cataloguing librarians, bibliographers and researchers who need fuller bibliographic information than may be provided in the "mini" record in the indexes and who have to find the register number in the index to consult this fuller data, and is wasteful of space because of the repetition of some bibliographic data and the necessity to repeat library location and holdings statements in both the register and the indexes.

While this new type of arrangement may become a model for national bibliographies, it is not yet recommended as a standard for union catalogues of serials. A practical sub-set of bibliographic information with holdings attached is preferable to an over-full master record and an over-abbreviated index, both of which require the location and holdings information for maximum utility.

8.1.6   *SUBJECT ACCESS*

The value of subject access to the majority of serial titles (as opposed to their contents) is not proven. Findings of studies[7] made on how users approach periodical literature indicate that, in 85 per cent of the cases, patrons are concerned with the physical address of a specific volume and issue of a title as cited in a reference, a footnote, a bibliography or an index. The unit requiring subject control is the article, paper or report contained in a serial, rather than the serial itself. For these reasons, the principal arrangement of, or access to, a union catalogue of serials is normally alphabetical by serial title.

If there is a pre-determined need for subject approach to a union catalogue of serials to further subject specialization plans, or for other purposes, which justifies the time and resources required to provide it, and if it can be supplied without sacrificing quality in the higher priority needs of the other sequences, it must still be borne in mind that, once-assigned, this access, also, requires up-dating to reflect the changing subject content of serials over the years and the evolution of disciplines.

There is at present no internationally-accepted standard for subject identification which covers the serials range from the very general to the very specific, and takes into account great national variations in cultural and linguistic traditions. Possibilities include subject headings, classification schemes in detailed sequence or broad subject divisions, coding, and key words and phrases, but none is entirely satisfactory for serials.

Machine-readable files offer more possibilities, including PRECIS with detailed controlled vocabulary and international exchange, made available through the development of multilingual thesauri; assigning multiple broad subject headings from a standard list, and retrieving records by more than one characteristic, or related subject headings if linked in the system. If multiple subject headings are provided together with a search capability which allows retrieval by each significant word and by any combination of significant words in the data base, the combined approach may provide greater subject access of value for some reference and selection purposes.

Coding systems representing a few hundred broad subject headings provide an inexpensive search capability for some types of serials such as periodicals and monographic series. Such systems are not sufficiently specific for all types of serials nor for all types of subject listings and searches. Should more specific subject delineation be needed for a particular application, the coding system should be supplemented by the assignation of fuller subject headings.

But access to words in titles and corporate bodies, and the use of descriptors, should not be considered as substitutes for subject access systems such as those provided by the indexing and abstracting data bases. Full text searching, and free text searching of words in abstracts, should be the aim of subject analysis of serial literature, i.e. the content of the serial, not the serial itself, should be the focus.

8.2 MICROFORM EDITIONS

The special problems of style, presentation and arrangement of microform editions are covered in 9.6.

8.3 ON-LINE DISPLAYS

The special problems of on-line systems and the multiple access points available are covered in 9.7.

8.4 Regardless of medium used, the page lay-out, typography and headings should be designed to facilitate use, understanding and readability of the union catalogue of serials.

Chapter 9
Criteria for Special Categories

9   The general principles provided in these *Guidelines* are valid for all types of union catalogues, but the wide variety of possibilities necessitates consideration of additional characteristics relevant to some special categories. This chapter considers the criteria to be borne in mind for the following types of material or types of union catalogues of serials:-

—Newspapers (see 9.1);
—Government publications (see 9.2);
—Conference proceedings (see 9.3);
—Subject bibliographies (see 9.4);
—Historical bibliographies (see 9.5);
—Microfiche editions (see 9.6);
—On-line systems (see 9.7).

9.1   *NEWSPAPERS*

Newspapers are primary reference and research sources. Because of their physical nature, they present storage and preservation problems. Union catalogues of newspapers provide an invaluable tool to inventory holdings, and the essential one to formulate and execute national acquisition and preservation programmes.

It is impractical to combine newspapers with other kinds of serials in the same union catalogue. The most efficient use of a newspaper catalogue depends upon a *geographic* arrangement, and of other kinds of serials upon a *title* arrangement. Special attention must be paid to the place(s) of publication, as the user is normally seeking historical information connected with a certain area, he may not know the precise title of the newspaper, and his search may be hampered by a multitude of commonly-used titles published simultaneously or chronologically in the same city, and by the many variations in titles which have occurred. The holdings statements also differ, because the user's approach is usually by *date,* and citations are rarely made to enumeration data (which are also subject to frequent change in systems, to mis-numberings and disruptions). More specific information is often needed for newspaper holdings.

Newspapers also present problems for the following reasons:-

(1) Insufficient attention has been devoted to them in existing cataloguing codes, which has led to overall lack of adequate bibliographic control.
(2) There is difficulty in defining the term "newspaper".
(3) They are not always included in national bibliographies, and the ethnic press, in particular, has been neglected.
(4) They are published in a multiplicity of variant editions unique to this type of serial: within each day; within each week; local, regional, national and international variants appearing simultaneously; formats; languages; types of microforms; duplicate microfilming ventures with different contents, etc.
(5) They frequently change their titles over a long period of time, and such changes may be either major or minor.
(6) They include inserts, and issue various kinds of supplements such as weekly (often syndicated) magazines, advertising, radio and television guides, comics, and special sections and cultural reviews, some of which may also be available by separate acquisition arrangements and may constitute separate serials.
(7) It is difficult to describe publishing responsibility, because of the succession of individuals and/or firms associated with each newspaper.
(8) It is difficult to determine what constitutes a complete file of a given title, and to establish the history in the absence of such a complete file.

Solution of these problems in a union catalogue environment is dependent on the employment of serials librarians with a special knowledge of newspaper bibliography and control, and an understanding of the inadequacies of existing national and international bibliographic systems.[8]

9.1.1   *GENERAL PRINCIPLES*

The following points should be given special consideration by compilers of union catalogues of newspapers:-

(1) The Introduction should include a clear definition of "newspaper" to indicate the scope (see 8.1.1 and 9.1.2).
(2) The primary arrangement should be geographic with a title index (see 9.1.5).
(3) Inkprint and microform newspapers should be covered in a single source, with separate bibliographic records for variant editions (see 6.6.1.1).
(4) It is considered impractical to attempt in this kind of tool to cover the publishing, printing and distribution history, and the political bias, of each newspaper.
(5) It may be advisable to catalogue under earliest, latest, best-known or longest-lived title, rather than successive entry (see 6.5.1.1), when insufficient history is available to describe the newpaper in successive segments and/or many title variations of very short duration or minor character have occurred.

9.1.2   *DEFINITIONS*

There is no internationally-accepted definition of a newspaper, but this kind of serial is usually printed originally on newsprint, in a format of not less than four columns of type per page, is issued at least once a month, without a cover, and has a masthead. It usually contains general news coverage, rather than being oriented towards specific subject matter, but certain special types such as financial, student, ethnic, etc., are common to many countries.

It is particularly important to ensure inclusion of newspapers produced by minority ethnic and language groups within a country, which often appear in languages and/or scripts different from those in general use. An ethnic newspaper is primarily intended for one or several ethnic, racial, cultural, or national groups, is issued in newspaper format, is usually edited and published within the particular community, and deals with a range of news topics that go beyond the reporting of activities of a particular organization or special interest group.

It is helpful in machine-readable files to include codes which identify both the *type of newspaper* and any *ethnic/cultural group* involved to facilitate the production of specialized bibliographies and information retrieval.

9.1.3 DATA ELEMENTS—BIBLIOGRAPHIC CONTROL

In addition to those listed in Chapter 6 (Bibliographic Control), a special data element—GEOGRAPHIC NAME ACCESS—is needed to provide an hierarchical form of geographic display of newspapers in the union catalogue and to accommodate problems with commonly-used titles. The recommended hierarchy is as follows:

(1) country;
(2) state; province; territory; republic, etc.;
(3) city; town; municipality; village; settlement; etc.

Data is required for *all* places in which the newspaper has been published, with additional access points provided for earlier and variant names of each country, state, city, etc. It is accordingly advisable to establish a geographic name authority file (see 6.2).

It may be helpful to include subject headings embodying geographic data, to cover the *region served* by the newspaper, as well as the place(s) of publication.

The general problems with cataloguing of microforms and reprints of serials, including newspapers, are discussed in 6.6.

9.1.4 DATA ELEMENTS—HOLDINGS CONTROL

Holdings should be described in terms of *chronology* (see 7.4.2.2), indicating any gaps or incompleteness by means of the standard symbols, or *retention statements* (see 7.6).

Particular attention should be paid to notes clarifying holdings (see 7.4.3). It is helpful for both acquisition and interlending purposes if information is given as to whether a microform held is a *master*, a *preservation master*, or a *service copy*.

It may be necessary to include data regarding months held as well as years, and to inventory individual issues of historical or archival value.

Holdings are even more useful when the locations include

private collections, historical societies and archives, press agencies, newspaper offices and micropublishers, and show the repository of the microform master.

Holdings of contemporary newspapers must be kept constantly up-to-date because of frequent changes caused by loss, deterioration, transfers or replacement by other editions.

9.1.5   *ARRANGEMENT*

The primary arrangement should be geographic by country, sub-arranged by state or province, etc., and further sub-arranged by city, town, etc. Within each locality, the newspapers should be listed alphabetically by title.

If the newspaper has been published in more than one place, the complete record should appear under *each* place of publication.

A title plus place(s) of publication index to the main geographic sequence is essential.

9.2   *GOVERNMENT PUBLICATIONS*

Government serials have frequently been omitted from union catalogues. Difficulties of distribution and acquisition, and of cataloguing material which frequently changes its issuing body, the sheer bulk of titles received on depository arrangements, and inadequate control of the publications of intergovernmental organizations, have led to collections which are barely identified, yet alone made available through location tools. Bibliographically, the serials governments publish do not differ substantially from other kinds of serials. Patrons do not think in terms of "non-government serials" and "government serials", but seek specific titles, whether distinctive or requiring issuing body for more precise identification. The "distinction between government and nongovernment serials is false and unwise when it results in uneven treatment. . .Serials are serials, no matter what the issuing body may be. . .On all counts it is desirable to treat documents like other serials. Substandard treatment is nothing less than a counsel of expediency."[9] The neglect can no longer be justified now that cataloguing copy is being made available in machine-readable national bibliographies, and government publishers themselves are beginning to contribute data to central agencies.

All official and semi-official serials produced by government ministries and departments, national councils and research institutes, etc., executive, judicial and legislative serials, as well as other types, should be included, with appropriate identification and summarized holdings, regardless of jurisdiction and level of government, i.e.:-

—Federal/national;
—State/provincial;
—County/departmental;
—Local;
—Multi-local;
—Intergovernmental;
—Government in exile or clandestine.

For union catalogues consisting solely of government serials, the preferred arrangement is *geographic by political jurisdiction,* and subsequently *by issuing agency,* with a *title index.* There should be separate listings for the publications of international intergovernmental organizations.

9.3 CONFERENCE PROCEEDINGS

The proceedings of *regular* meetings of organizations should be included in union catalogues of serials. Proceedings of other conferences, symposia, seminars and meetings are difficult to retrieve from such tools, and are best handled as monographs to bring out any subject interest and to facilitate retrieval under variant conference names, theme and generic titles, editors, sponsors, etc., as these change from issue to issue. It may be desirable to report all conference proceedings to a special union catalogue including works of all conferences, both those held once only and those held periodically.

9.4 SUBJECT BIBLIOGRAPHIES

It is not a function of union catalogues of serials to provide systematic and informative subject bibliographies. The problems of subject access to serials generally are covered in Chapter 8 (Recommended Standards for Style, Presentation and Arrangement).

Broad subject groupings in the humanities and social sciences, or in science and technology, are not recommended because of difficulties in the allocation of general materials and other serials of interest to more than one such area. Similarly, the breaking-down of barriers between conventional subject fields, and the trend in research to become more interdisciplinary, are resulting in the publication of more serials that are multidisciplinary or interdisciplinary in content and/or use. These factors dictate that union catalogues be either comprehensive in coverage or restricted to a narrow subject.

The latter will frequently coincide with the interests of a special network or close-knit group of libraries representing well-defined subjects, such as music or law. Such catalogues may be self-sufficient for selection and reference purposes for those working in the narrow discipline, and obviate the necessity for more general tools. In other instances, such specific subject catalogues may supplement general ones by providing more depth and being more comprehensive and including all types of libraries specializing in the field, so that the user is shown both the large and small institutions in a geographic area in which the serial resources needed for the study of the subject may be found. This assists in-depth searching by inter-library-loan offices, while the strengths and weaknesses of collections thus revealed may facilitate co-operative subject specialization schemes.

It may be possible for such subject catalogues to be produced from a larger data base if an appropriate approach has been provided in the latter (see 8.1.6 and 11.2). Subject union catalogues should not be specially compiled unless there is a demonstrated need and they can be justified economically. If subject catalogues proliferate, they result in more data banks to which to report (unless they are a by-product of a more comprehensive system), and an increase in the number of potential reference sources to be consulted by interlending personnel.

9.5 *HISTORICAL BIBLIOGRAPHIES*

Union catalogues of serials which are also scholarly historical bibliographies add extra dimensions to the standard product. They can reveal the evolution of a subject; shed light on social, political, literary, scientific or historical thought; cover periods, regions, languages and types of serials not yet included elsewhere; inventory early or suppressed newspapers and other serials; or display the state of preservation of serials from confiscated publishing houses, or deliberately destroyed or lost in disasters; or help to trace the history of a national periodical or newspaper press.

Period union catalogues have sometimes been specially created because traditional ones have been time-consuming to search in this respect. The MARC-Serials formats offer coding to facilitate such an approach, and on-line services may be able to limit searches by date.

Whatever the arrangement used for such bibliographies, there must be access by title, and all general principles relating to bibliographic and holdings information apply.

The body of the material covered for specialized serials of this nature in the humanities tends to remain of permanent value and leads to a certain stability in this type of tool. Reported holdings remain useful for long periods, particularly for material published prior to 1850/75, and frequently-issued editions are only necessary if reprints or microforms become available. Bibliographies which report holdings of material subsequent to this period require more frequent up-dating because of the impact of deterioration, which erodes the validity of the holdings statements.

Such bibliographies are particularly valuable for reference work and as guides for acquiring older serials.

MICROFICHE EDITIONS

9.6 A high-quality microfiche edition illustrates the feasibility of microforms as reference tools. The ideal COM union catalogue should not only constitute well-organized bibliography but should reflect new technological capabilities with due regard to pertinent standards. Individual idiosyncrasies in the compilation and presentation of microform editions of union catalogues of serials are even more inimical to their successful use than those in printed versions.

9.6.1 International micrographics standards contribute to the free flow and sharing of information across national borders, but such standardization is presently lacking in numerous respects.

Until standards for physical characteristics, headers, page and record formats, indexing, image-quality and legibility control, etc., become available through the work of the appropriate ISO committees of experts, adherence to the following principles is recommended:-

(1) The fiche edition itself should be given adequate bibliographic identification on a separate title-frame (see 8.1).
(2) The microfiche headers should be eye-readable and include the following bibliographic information:-

—ISSN;
—title of fiche edition;
—edition statement and date;
—type of sequence (title, issuing body, etc.);
—span covered (first and last entries on each fiche);
—number of each fiche in the set.

(3) Multiple sequences should be explained in the Introduction and should be physically differentiated by the use of coloured headers or film.
(4) The Introduction should be on a separate fiche, preferably including all material which would appear in a printed edition, but giving at least the essentials if space is limited.
(5) Index fiche should give a brief explanation of the indexing system.
(6) A separate eye-readable conventional print Introduction or User's Manual should be provided to prevent user difficulties in referring back to an explanatory fiche while viewing another in equipment lacking a dual carrier, and to offset any space limitations for introductory material on the fiche itself.
(7) The reduction ratio should be specified. (1:48 is presently a widely used standard, with 1:42 as the second most common.)
(8) A "micro" test object should be included for use in evaluating the performance of the microfiche reading equipment.

Scroll formats in continuous columns, with running heads at the top and bottom of each column to aid users in locating specific headings on the fiche, are considered preferable to frames oriented in either a comic strip or cine mode with an index on each fiche, because they are easier to use and pack information more efficiently.

If a scroll format is not used, a finding-aid should be provided, either separately or in the explanatory material, to show the grid pattern in which the micro-images are positioned.

A title card is helpful in fiche packaged in plastic sleeves. Envelopes, easel binders, and other types of fiche containers and organizers, should carry appropriate identification.

Particular attention should be paid to those features which contribute to ease of use, including lay-out (such as avoiding splitting of records over columns, or fiche pages, or individual fiche), print quality, legible labelling and ensuring good readability under magnification.

The archival quality of the microfiche is not normally relevant, since each issue usually supersedes the previous. Vesicular or diazo film is therefore suitable for most purposes.

In all other respects, the COM edition should coincide with the printed equivalent.

9.7 ON-LINE SYSTEMS

An on-line union catalogue of serials which embodies all the best features of traditional systems, combined with quality control, not only results in well-organized bibliography, but adds new dimensions for both librarians and patrons through enhanced technological capabilities, particularly the possibility of continuous file modification. The use of search keys, and key term and phrase searching, offers an inexpensive alternative to traditional access to bibliographic data.

9.7.1.1 A separate User's Manual should be provided which contains the following:-

(1) The same information as for printed and fiche editions, including an explanation of all types of data displayed on the screen.

(2) System-specific information and search aids:-

—specifications for communicating with the computer;
—summary of operator commands/requests;
—summary of display options available;
—summary of search keys available;
—techniques of efficient searching, step by step;
—explanation of computer responses;
—sample searches;
—list of any codes, abbreviations, etc., used;
—definition of subject scheme used, or list of subjects if unique to the system.

9.7.1.2 In addition, training sessions are needed to teach the patron the mechanics of approaching and performing a search, and logic and strategies to achieve an efficient and economical performance level. Elementary directions for self-instructed lessons should include an introduction to and description of the terminal keyboard, and explanations on how to do various types of searches. Step-by-step on-line instruction packages should also be provided.

9.7.2 *DISPLAY FORMATS*

A variety of display formats is possible in an on-line system. Provision should be made for the following as a minimum:-

(1) Initial default display of a *mini* bibliographic record for each discrete bibliographic unit in the file, with full display of all reported holdings to the same standard as in printed and fiche editions. (A mini record is understood to contain all those elements specified in 6.3.3.)
(2) The option of subsequent display of the *full* bibliographic record if the mini record has been extracted from the more comprehensive librarian's type of catalogue.
(3) Display under each corporate responsibility of the titles associated with that body, with information in 1) and 2) as above.
(4) Display of the complete history and holdings of each serial under first, successive and latest entries.

9.7.3 *CAPABILITIES*

The on-line union catalogue of serials should be accessible at all hours the institution is open.

The following capabilities are also regarded as highly desirable:-

—Rapid response time.
—Consultation of the union serials file without necessity of prior scanning of a succession of indexes to eliminate non-serial material.
—Use of Boolean logic operators to permit combination of values for several indexes in one search request.
—Ability to limit searches by date, medium, language or place of publication.
—Browsable mode to refine imprecise searching.
—Key word capability.

9.7.3.1   Key word capability allowing the manipulation of natural language terms without thesaurus control is a particularly valuable and inexpensive access. It enables an item to be identified by the most significant words of its title and/or corporate body, thus facilitating access when the precise full citation is unknown and reducing user dependence on a knowledge of cataloguing rules, and may enhance any form of subject approach which has been provided.

9.7.4   *ACCESS POINTS*

The following are considered the minimum acceptable access points to the bibliographic record:-

— ISSN;
— national bibliography control numbers;
— precise title;
— key words and phrases from all titles and corporate bodies (and in any subject fields if this approach is desired).

Quick and direct access should be provided by established search keys and control numbers for the sophisticated user, while another level should be provided for the learner in the form of a prompting or "menu selection" technique.

Chapter 10

Responsibilities

10   As has been noted in Chapter 1 (General), the creation of a successful union catalogue of serials is a co-operative enterprise in which both the editorial centre and the contributors have well-defined responsibilities.

10.1   *RESPONSIBILITIES OF EDITORS*

There must be a strong and active union catalogue staff with the necessary professional training and experience to edit both bibliographic and holdings data, to assume responsibility for adherence to standards, consistency of approach and accuracy, and to exercise *quality control* in all respects as records are updated on a continuing basis.

10.1.1   Specific responsibilities of such a central agency include the following:-

—The design of the system, the generation of functional specifications, and the arrangements for the use of appropriate hardware and software.
—The formulation and maintenance of a detailed written editorial policy, including scope, cataloguing rules and procedures, and holdings standards.
—The establishment and monitoring of quantity and quality standards for bibliographic and holdings data required from participants, and the application of uniform standards and procedures throughout the network.
—The creation, management and maintenance of the complete data base.
—The establishment and maintenance of a sound filing system.
—The establishment and maintenance of authority files for

corporate and geographic names, uniform titles, and institutional symbols.
—The preparation, distribution and maintenance of internal editing, coding and procedural manuals.
—The preparation, distribution and maintenance of all necessary documentation to be supplied to contributors, including reporting instructions, definitions, standards to be followed, worksheets, and examples.
—The holding of meetings with appropriate staff from participating institutions, the supply of field representatives, the giving of workshops, and the training of appropriate personnel as and when necessary.
—The scheduling and organization of each library's input, with regular follow-up to maintain up-to-date and accurate records.
—The training of personnel in the editorial office to interpret reports received and standardize them.
—The verification and authentication of all bibliographic information submitted, either from the actual material, a surrogate, or a high-quality primary source of serials cataloguing data.
—The consolidation and editing of all contributed bibliographic data into a single, comprehensive, consistent and up-to-date record for each serial title, with resolution of all conflicts arising from the use of different formats, cataloguing codes and concepts, and policies on change of title.
—The review of all holdings reports submitted for consistency with standards, and the editing of them into meaningful display, including the adjustment of segments in accordance with the policy on changes of title, and the updating of all appropriate data when a serial dies.
—The transmission of problem lists to contributing libraries for further checking, verification, or reconciliation of discrepancies.
—The organization of all data in an arrangement which minimizes the number of sequences to be consulted by the user and maximizes the access points.
—The proof-reading of the master file for errors, duplications and inconsistencies, before arranging for the desired output.
—The production of the union catalogue in the preferred media format(s), accompanied by appropriate explanatory material.

—The publication and distribution of printed and fiche editions, including the deposit of copies with the national bibliographic agency.
—The preparation of guides to educate users of fiche and on-line systems.
—The arrangements for extraction of data from, and transmission of data to, other serials data bases, both to build up the union catalogue and to interface with similar serials projects at appropriate levels.
—The consultation as necessary with other experts in serials control, with computing and subject specialists, etc.
—The co-ordination of policies and development with the editors of appropriate monographic data bases.

10.2 *RESPONSIBILITIES OF CONTRIBUTORS*

Participating institutions should, wherever possible, assign an experienced serials librarian to co-ordinate and supervise the data gathering and submission. This librarian should ensure that the instructions of the central union catalogue agency are followed, maintain quality control at the institutional level, and see that accurate contributions in respect of new, changed and deleted records are forwarded on a regular and continuing basis.

The most effective structure for serials management purposes, including the most favourable environment for union catalogue functions, is one in which all serials-related activities are grouped together, because of reciprocal interdependence, into one unit for the benefit of maximum co-ordination, i.e. the *unified serials department*.[10]

10.2.1 Contributing libraries may be required to provide cataloguing copy for uniquely-held titles or titles not previously recorded in the central files or recorded with limited information. Surrogates will normally be requested to enable the central authenticating agency to undertake definitive cataloguing, but, by prior arrangement, individual libraries with a reputation for excellence in serials cataloguing may be designated to create original records on behalf of the system or to up-date bibliographic information therein. Some libraries may be designated as centres of responsibility for authenticating certain categories of serial records or participating in the establishment of authority files.

10.2.2   The method of submission of both cataloguing and holdings data will vary, as has been indicated in Chapter 5 (Compilation). While contributors may be able to input by submitting cards, slips, typed or printed lists, computer print-outs, etc., it is more efficient for the editorial office to supply preformatted worksheets and up-date forms for completion or review of previous reports. More sophisticated systems will expect to receive data via direct tape exchange or on-line terminal input.

10.2.3   Ideally, the individual library's own serials system should be MARC-compatible, and the same core of bibliographic data should be used for internal and networking purposes by interfacing with other MARC-structured serials files. Local serials data bases should include the appropriate fields to enable contributors to submit at least control numbers and summarized specific holdings statements, and preferably the full data element sets specified in Chapter 6 (Bibliographic Control) and Chapter 7 (Holdings Control).

10.2.4   Contributing libraries should ensure that adequate resources are made available to maintain a current and precise inventory of holdings, and see that revised holdings statements are submitted to the central agency on a regular basis as serial files are strengthened, withdrawn, or replaced by reprints and microforms.

Chapter 11

Output

11.1   *DISTRIBUTION*

In producing a union catalogue of serials, the agency responsible becomes a publisher. All the necessary information concerning distribution and availability of the union catalogue should be included on the verso of the title-page (see 8.1).

Copies of each edition should be forwarded to the national bibliographic agency. This will ensure that the existence of the union catalogue is made known to the national and international library community, will comply with any copyright and legal deposit obligations, and also help to avoid unnecessary duplication of union catalogue of serials activities.

11.2   *BY-PRODUCTS*

A machine-readable serials data base offers a bibliography-building capability, and the possibility of multiple by-products and sub-files, in magnetic tapes, COM catalogues, and printouts, either on a regular basis or on-demand, according to need.

Some of these possibilities are as follows:-

—Bibliographies of new serial titles.
—Bibliographies of critical titles.
—Bibliographies of microform masters.
—Broad subject catalogues.
—Catalogues of titles covered by one or more of the indexing and abstracting services.
—Selective catalogues by type of library, consortium, region, type of serial, period, etc.
—Indexes by corporate body, ISSN, key words, etc.

Such special bibliographic and sub-files are produced by searching the data base by one field, or by a combination of fields. It is axiomatic that, in order to obtain these products, the likely required parameters must be defined, and the necessary data collected and encoded in the records.

11.3 INDIVIDUAL LIBRARY CATALOGUE BY-PRODUCTS

It may sometimes be possible to produce institutional serials catalogues from a union catalogue, but the constraints of uniformity inherent in the latter may conflict with locally required individuality, may produce references to segments and related titles not held by a particular library, and reflect holdings editing at the central agency unacceptable to the institution concerned. Furthermore, library-specific information beyond location symbol and summarized holdings for one copy is best maintained at the local level.

If an individual catalogue is to be produced from a central file, all deviant entries must be maintained and associated with both the institution and its holdings statements.

11.4 INTELLECTUAL LEVEL BY-PRODUCTS

As an aid in selection, it may be useful to include in the bibliographic record a code denoting the intellectual level of the serial (that is, whether intended for children, general use, university, etc.). To satisfy this requirement, IFLA has developed the *International Target Audience Code* (ITAC) which may be used to provide serial listings by intellectual level of publication.

11.5 GEOGRAPHIC BY-PRODUCTS

The use of a country code (such as ISO 3166) has particular value in mechanized systems to identify the country of publication of each serial and produce area listings.

A geographic area code has been developed by the Library of Congress and can be used to indicate the region covered by a serial.

11.6 LANGUAGE BY-PRODUCTS

Language listings can be provided if the language(s) of the serial have been coded. ISO has prepared an international standard (ISO 639) which may be used for this purpose.

Chapter 12

Relationships with Other Systems

12   In order not to clutter union catalogues with details which are better handled in other ways, particularly data which is highly changeable, the relationship with other types of serial control systems should be carefully considered. The aim should be to include in the union catalogue only information of universal interest which furthers its primary functions. At the same time, technological developments and standardization in library systems interconnection must be borne in mind in anticipation of the time when union catalogues will be linked to other segments in the information sector.

12.1   CENTRAL SERIALS RECORDS

A union catalogue should not attempt to perform the functions of an institutional central serials record. The latter is more suited to the maintenance of institution-specific and copy-specific details and day-to-day management data which are essentially local and have very high transaction levels.

12.1.1   Such functions include the following:-

—Piece-by-piece recording of holdings, with all enumeration and chronology data; issue variants; special issues; supplements; detachable materials; serials within serials; title-pages, contents and indexes; cumulative indexes; and detailing of all changes in frequency, in number of volumes per year, number of issues per volume, etc.
—Local processing information, including condition; binding; routing; number of physical volumes or microfilm reels held; disposal instructions; issues out-of-print; "wants"; etc.

—Very specific location information, e.g. individual departments or offices.
—Local call numbers or shelf marks.

12.1.2 The central serials record is nonetheless closely interrelated with the union catalogue, since it provides the complete ongoing collation of each serial on which the bibliographic history is built, and the detailed holdings information from which each institutional report should be summarized. An effective union catalogue of serials is built on a firm base of serials record-keeping at the institutional level, but in turn it requires recourse to the central serials records in the individual institution for enumerative and other daily processing data.

12.2 *OTHER BIBLIOGRAPHIC LEVELS*

It is recognized that serials constitute one of four bibliographic levels:

monograph
collection
serial
analytic

which have relationships. Because of the special problems they present and the special treatment they require, serials and newspapers are most frequently recorded in separate systems. These files should be compatible with those for other bibliographic levels, and made available through generalized search routines in a total catalogue access system which accepts records of all kinds of library materials and processes them in a uniform way.

12.2.1 While monographic series are recommended for inclusion in union catalogues of serials, and specific holdings should be reported by appropriate sequential designations under series title, it is understood that analytics should be reported to data banks of monographic information. In this way, both the serial and monographic aspects of this type of material will be controlled. Whether the user's citation is to author/title or series, the information can be retrieved from the appropriate data banks, which in turn can be co-ordinated by use of the ISSN for the series.

12.3 NATIONAL BIBLIOGRAPHY

The union catalogue of serials may be partially created from a national bibliography (see 6.3.3.1), but in countries without a national bibliography, it may itself have to serve as the serials section. The serial bibliographic records of an entire nation may not be contained in a single data base, but in a number of files, such as those of regional resource networks, national periodical lending collections, and major research libraries. Together, these form the nation's serials records, and, if these resources are shown as a whole in a union catalogue, a form of national serials bibliography results.

The union catalogue of serials may often be more useful than the national bibliography when it contains the following:-

—Titles published prior to the issuing of the national bibliography.
—Titles which have undergone some kind of change since they appeared in the national bibliography, and revised records have not been included in the latter.
—Categories of serials which have been omitted from the national bibliography because the compilers have considered them unsuitable for inclusion therein.

12.4 INDEXING AND ABSTRACTING SERVICES

As has already been indicated (see 2.6), on-line services provide a system of links beginning with the patron's literature search to produce citations, the consultation of an individual library catalogue, and then the perusal of other union catalogues to locate the specific title and specific issue, resulting in an on-line inter-library-loan request to the holding institution beyond the confines of the user's own geographic region.

Techniques are being developed to link related records in library files and those of the indexing and abstracting services. It is desirable that the same or similar techniques be used in union catalogues of serials and in the services which index and abstract serial publications, so that the user is able not only to find a serial item which suits his needs cited in such a service, but to locate readily an appropriate holding institution. Designers of union catalogues of serials in machine-readable form should therefore allow a field for machine identification of the control numbers of related records in indexing and abstracting services, as well as sufficient bibliographic information concerning the related record for human identification.

12.5 SERIALS DIRECTORIES

A union catalogue should not attempt to perform the functions of a serials directory. The latter is more suited to conveying the following types of information, most of which constitute highly volatile data elements and can only be kept constantly up-to-date by the serial publishers themselves through frequently published new editions or in an on-line service:-

—Full names and addresses of publishers and distributors.
—Terms of availability.
—Forms of issue.
—Pricing rates and structures.
—Coverage by indexing and abstracting services.

12.6 OTHER PUBLISHERS' FILES

Serials systems which include such access points as *documents classification numbers* issued by government agencies at all levels, other *stock numbers* such as those in use with technical reports, will facilitate institutional ordering and suppliers' stock control in future. These numbers are not considered essential in the union catalogue of serials environment.

The names of *commercial* publishers have not been recommended for display because this is a very rarely used access point. It is not normally included in citations, and is an element which frequently changes over a period of time as serial publications are sold to another firm or the name of the firm itself changes. The lists and catalogues of the commercial publishers should be left to provide this little-used information.

12.7 DIRECTORIES OF LIBRARIES

Since a union catalogue gives the names and addresses of the contributing institutions, it may also serve as a library directory. This is not a primary function, and the inclusion of such institutional information should not be regarded as a substitute for creating new, or contributing to existing, directories of libraries.

12.8 CHRONOLOGICAL CONCORDANCES

Given the difficulties of describing the holdings of the majority of serials in chronological terms, tables which correlate chronological and numerical data for each title are useful tools which are sometimes included in union catalogues. This medium is not considered suitable for the purpose. It is suggested serial publishers should create and maintain data banks displaying enumeration/chronology relationships for each of their serial titles, which might eventually become available through Open Systems Interconnection (see 12.9).

12.9 UNION CATALOGUES OF SERIALS WITHIN THE BROADER CONTEXT OF THE INFORMATION TRANSFER CHAIN

Bibliographic, location and holdings data exchange can no longer be considered in a vacuum. The library community is only one segment of the information sector. It is now recognized that automated library systems must interface with outside information systems. Network architecture is being developed which will eventually interconnect libraries, bibliographic centres, the information production and dissemination industry, the publishing industry, ordering/distributing networks, and home information systems.

Creators of union catalogues of serials must therefore bear in mind progress towards the provision of a common basis of coordination of standards development for the purpose of systems interconnection.

Efforts to facilitate data interchange amongst autonomous systems should take place within the framework of the common functions and procedures known as Open Systems Interconnection (OSI). Progenitors of new union catalogues of serials should support the concept of open access and work towards the removal of barriers to inter-systems communication and adopt common communication conventions, such as command language, standards of patron identification, address numbers, lending terms, etc., as these are developed by the appropriate standardizing organizations, in addition to adhering to those already developed by the library community for communicating bibliographic, location and holdings data in an internationally acceptable format. Mutual recognition and use of all the relevant communication protocols and standards will eventually make possible the maximum use of network resources, which, in turn, will make a major contribution towards the ultimate goals of both Universal Bibliographic Control and Universal Availability of Publications.

References for Guidelines

1. See, e.g., L. Brummel, *Union Catalogues: Their Problems and Organization* (Paris: UNESCO, 1956).
2. See: *Canadian MARC Communication Format: Mini-MARC* (Ottawa: National Library of Canada, 1975-   ).
3. *Ibid.*
4. See, e.g., Elizabeth Pan, *Library Serials Control Systems: A Literature Review and Bibliography* (Washington, D.C.: ERIC Clearinghouse on Library and Information Sciences, 1970), p. 8, 28.
5. *Guidelines for ISDS* (Paris: UNESCO, 1973).
6. See: *Canadian MARC Communication Format: Mini-MARC.*
7. Pan, *Library Serials Control Systems,* p. 8, 28.
8. See: Hana Komorous, "Union Catalogue of Newspapers in British Columbia Libraries", *Serials Librarian* 3, no. 3 (Spring 1979), pp. 255-288, for a recent attempt to solve these problems in terms of a special expansion of the *Canadian MARC Communication Format: Mini-MARC.*
9. Andrew D. Osborn, *Serial Publications: Their Place and Treatment in Libraries.* 2d rev. ed. (Chicago: American Library Association, 1973), pp. 58-59.
10. See, e.g., Mitsuko Collver, "Organization of Serials Work for Manual and Automated Systems", *Library Resources and Technical Services,* 24, no. 4 (Fall 1980), pp. 307-316.

Part 2

APPENDIXES

Appendix I
Definition of a Serial and Types of Serials

A. *DEFINITION OF A SERIAL*

A serial is:

"A publication in print or in non-print form, issued in successive parts, usually having numerical or chronological designations, and intended to be continued indefinitely. Serials include periodicals, newspapers, annuals (reports, yearbooks, directories, etc.), journals, memoirs, proceedings, transactions etc., of societies, and monographic series."

B. *TYPES OF SERIALS*

Serials may be published in either print or non-print form, and may therefore exist in many formats and media, including original, reprint, facsimile, photocopy, microform, multi-media kit, sound recording, video-recording, etc.

The following types of materials should be included in union catalogues of serials, providing they are *serially published:*-

—administrative reports
—almanacs
—annuals
—bibliographies
—bulletins
—catalogues
—college and university catalogues and calendars
—company reports
—conference and congress proceedings
—directories
—financial statements
—gazettes
—gift books
—guide books

—handbooks
—house organs
—indexing and abstracting services
—international organization publications
—journals
—law reports
—laws and statutes
—lists
—looseleaf services
—memoirs
—monographic serials
—monographic series
—newsletters
—newspapers
—parliamentary papers
—patents
—periodicals
—proceedings
—progress reports
—standards
—statistics
—tables
—technical reports
—timetables
—transactions
—yearbooks

It is understood that these types of serials should be included regardless of by whom published, i.e. the serial publications of all kinds of educational, cultural, scientific and technical organizations, legal and governmental bodies, fraternal, labour, business and religious organizations, and all kinds of societies and associations, should be reported to union catalogues of serials.

Appendix II
Glossary and Abbreviations

A. *GLOSSARY OF SIGNIFICANT TERMS*

ACCESS POINT — A name, term, code, etc., under which a bibliographic record may be searched and identified.

AUTHORITY FILE — A file that contains records of the authorized form of corporate body, meeting and conference names; and uniform title, geographic, series, and subject headings. Cross references and notes are usually included where appropriate. Such records in an automated authority file may or may not be linked to the bibliographic data base.

BIBLIOGRAPHIC RECORD — The logically related data elements which collectively represent the information concerning a bibliographic work.

BIBLIOGRAPHIC UNIT — A logical segment of the publication sequence of a serial as designated by the publisher, e.g. an issue, edition, etc.

BIBLIOGRAPHIC UTILITY — An organization that maintains large on-line bibliographic data bases and provides products and services related to these bases to its customers/members.

BOOLEAN OPERATORS — AND, OR, NOT, NOR. These operators are a technique for customizing a search request by combining or excluding characters, words, and numbers.

CAPTION — A word attached as a prefix to the enumerative data describing its type, e.g. volume, tome, Band, etc.

CENTRAL SERIALS RECORD	A total serials holdings record of a library system, usually in one sequence, consisting of an enumerative statement of current issues, consolidated into summarized information concerning volumes and years held, to provide a retrospective volume-by-volume inventory. Combined with acquisition, claiming, processing and binding data, such a record presents the optimum for institutional control of serials.
CHRONOLOGY	The dating system or systems used by the publisher to identify the individual bibliographic unit, e.g. nominal date, date of coverage, date of publication, etc.
COMMUNICATIONS FORMAT	A format generally accepted by a number of data processing facilities for the purpose of transferring data or records from one centre to another in a consistent manner.
COMMUNICATIONS PROTOCOL	A formal set of conventions governing the format and relative timing of message exchanges between two computers.
CORPORATE BODY	An organization or group of persons that is identified by a particular name and that acts, or may act, as an entity. Typical examples of corporate bodies are associations, institutions, business firms, non-profit enterprises, government agencies, religious bodies, local churches and conferences.
DATA ELEMENT	A distinguishable, defined unit of information.
DISPLAY	The presentation of data for human interpretation.
ENUMERATION	The numerical system or systems used by the publisher on the bibliographic unit to distinguish one unit from another, one volume from another, etc.
FIELD	A specified area in a record used for a particular category of data, e.g. location of title proper or ISSN information.
FORMAT (a)	Any particular physical presentation of a bibliographic entity.

FORMAT (b)	(Machine-readable data files). A predetermined order or arrangement of data in a record.
GAP	A break in the sequence of enumeration and/or chronology of a serial holding indicating a volume, issue or date not held.
GENERAL MATERIAL DESIGNATION	A term indicating the broad class of material to which an item belongs, e.g. microform, sound recording, etc.
HARDWARE	Physical computer equipment.
HEADING	A name, word, or phrase placed at the head of a catalogue entry to provide an access point in the catalogue.
HOLDINGS STATEMENT	A record of the bibliographic units of a specific serial held by a specific institution or collection.
KEY-TITLE	The unique name assigned to a serial by the International Serials Data System.
MAGNETIC TAPE	A tape with a magnetic surface on which machine-readable data, such as records in the MARC-Serials format, can be stored.
MARC-SERIALS FORMAT	A machine-readable cataloguing and exchange format for serials data, developed by the Library of Congress.
MICROFICHE	A sheet of film bearing a number of micro-images in two-dimensional array.
MICROFILM	A length of film bearing a number of micro-images in linear array.
MICROFORM	A generic term for any medium, transparent or opaque, bearing micro-images.
MICROFORM MASTER	One which is used only to make copies and from which single copies are normally available for purchase at any time.
MICROFORM PRESERVATION MASTER	One which meets the definition of a master microform, but is usually housed in a temperature-controlled, fire-proof place.
MICROFORM SERVICE COPY	One which is made available for use by readers.

MONOGRAPH	A non-serial item, i.e. an item either complete in one part or complete, or intended to be completed, in a finite number of separate parts.
NOMINAL DATE	The date associated with identification data for a volume, issue, etc.
ON-LINE	Direct user interrogation of, or input to, the computer containing the data base, via a terminal and a telephone line.
REFERENCE	A direction from one heading or entry to another.
ROMANIZATION	Conversion of names or text not written in the Roman alphabet to Roman alphabet form.
SEARCH KEY	A unique set of characters, formed by following a specific rule, input via a terminal to conduct a search.
SERIAL	See *APPENDIX I* for definition.
SOFTWARE	The control programmes or instructions used to make a computer perform its intended functions.
TERMINAL	A device for sending and receiving information over a communication channel, often equipped with a television picture tube to display data visually.
TITLE PROPER	The chief name of a serial including any alternative title, but excluding parallel titles and other title information.
UNIFORM TITLE	A title used to identify a serial, to file it, and to link its bibliographic segments, when its title proper is identical to the title proper of another serial in the same catalogue or data base.

B. *ABBREVIATIONS AND ACRONYMS*

COM	Computer-output-microform.
CONSER	*Con*version of *Ser*ials Project.
CRT	Cathode ray tube. A *terminal* with a television picture tube to display information visually.

IFLA	International Federation of Library Associations and Institutions.
ISBD(S)	International Standard Bibliographic Description for Serials.
ISDS	International Serials Data System.
ISO	International Organization for Standardization.
ISSN	International Standard Serial Number.
ITAC	International Target Audience Code.
LC/MARC	Library of Congress MARC.
MARC	*Ma*chine-*r*eadable *c*ataloguing.
OSI	Open Systems Interconnection.
PRECIS	Preserved Context Indexing System.
SDI	Selective dissemination of information.
UAP	Universal Availability of Publications.
UBC	Universal Bibliographic Control.
UNIMARC	MARC International Format.
UNISIST	Intergovernmental Programme for Co-operation in the field of Scientific and Technological Information.

Appendix III
Summary of Essential Bibliographic and Holdings Data Elements

	ALL SERIALS EXCEPT NEWSPAPERS	NEWSPAPERS
PRIMARY ARRANGEMENT	TITLE	GEOGRAPHIC
BIBLIOGRAPHIC CONTROL DATA ELEMENTS	Uniform Title Title Proper General Material Designation Corporate Body Edition Statement Numeric/Chronological Designation Place of Publication Notes: 1. Linking 2. Clarifying Holdings 3. Describing Microform/Reprint Variations ISSN = Key-Title National Bibliography Control and Retrieval Numbers	Uniform Title Title Proper General Material Designation Corporate Body Edition Statement Numeric/Chronological Designation Place(s) of Publication Geographic Name Access Notes: 1. Linking 2. Clarifying Holdings 3. Describing Microform/Reprint Variations ISSN = Key-Title National Bibliography Control and Retrieval Numbers
HOLDINGS CONTROL DATA ELEMENTS	Ownership Symbol Series/Volumes/Numbers Held Dates Held	Ownership Symbol Dates Held

	ALL SERIALS EXCEPT NEWSPAPERS	NEWSPAPERS
PRIMARY ARRANGEMENT	TITLE	GEOGRAPHIC
	Retention Statement	Retention Statement
	Notes:	Notes:
	1. Microform Polarity 2. Clarifying Edition Held	1. Microform Polarity 2. Clarifying Edition Held
	Local System Control Number	Local System Control Number
	Date of Report	Date of Report

Part 3

SUPPLEMENT:

LIST OF TITLES COVERED BY THE INTERNATIONAL SURVEY

Section 1
International Lists

Contributing Countries

U.S./Canada	Union list of periodicals for the cities of Sault Ste. Marie, Ontario, and Sault Ste. Marie, Michigan.
U.S./Canada	Union list of military periodicals.
various	International union list of Communist Chinese serials: scientific, technical and medical with selected social science titles.
various	Bibliography of Chinese newspapers and periodicals in European libraries.
various	3,200 revues et journaux arabes de 1800 à 1965.
Belgium/Luxembourg	Catalogue collectif belge et luxembourgeois des périodiques étrangers en cours de publication.
S. Africa/U.S./U.K.	South African newspapers available on microfilm.
various	Deutsche Zeitungsbestände in Bibliotheken und Archiven.
Kenya/Uganda/Tanzania	Union list of periodicals in East African libraries.
various	Union catalogue of learned periodical publications in South Asia.

Scandinavia	Periodicals of interest to American studies; a selected checklist of holdings in Nordic libraries.
Malaysia/U.K./Singapore	Bibliography of Malay and Arabic periodicals published in the Straits Settlements and Peninsular Malay States 1876-1941, with an annotated union list of holdings.
S. Africa/Rhodesia/Basutoland	Anthropological and archaeological journals in South African libraries.
Fiji/Western Samoa/New Caledonia	South Pacific union list of periodicals.
Kuwait/Iraq/Saudi Arabia	Regional union list of scientific and technical periodicals in the Gulf Area.
various	Periodicals for South-East Asian studies; a union catalogue of holdings in British and selected European libraries.
U.S./Canada	Undergrounds; a union list of alternative periodicals in libraries of the United States and Canada.
various	Ontario ethno-cultural newspapers, 1835-1972.
various	Burmese and Thai newspapers; an international union list.
U.K./Eire	Union list of periodicals in the Romance languages and literatures in British national, university and special libraries.
U.K./U.S./Australia	Bibliography of British newspapers: Wiltshire.

U.K./Eire	American newspaper holdings in British and Irish libraries.
Eire/Ulster	Union list of current periodicals and serials in Irish libraries.
U.K./Eire	Check-list of Japanese periodicals held in British university and research libraries.
various	Periodicals in Eastern African libraries.
various	AGLINET union list of serials.
U.S./Canada/U.K./Eire	Index and finding list of serials published in the British Isles, 1789-1832.
U.S./Canada/U.K./Eire	Britain's theatrical periodicals, 1720-1967.
U.S./U.K./Eire	Descriptive finding list of unstamped British periodicals, 1830-1836.
U.S./Canada	African newspapers in selected American libraries; a union list.
U.S./Canada	List of the serial publications of foreign governments, 1815-1931.
U.S./Canada	Half a century of Soviet serials, 1917-1968; a bibliography and union list of serials published in the U.S.S.R.
U.S./Canada	American newspapers, 1821-1936; a union list.
various	History and bibliography of American newspapers, 1690-1820.

U.K./Eire	Hand-list of Irish newspapers, 1685-1750.
Scandinavia	List agr.
various	Periodicals in Southern African libraries (PISAL).
Turkey/France	Eski harfli türkçe süreli yayinlar toplu kataloğu.
various	Union list of Pacific imprint serials held in Pacific libraries.
U.S./U.K.	Almanacs of the United States.
various	Ethnic newspapers and periodicals in Michigan; a checklist.
U.K./U.S./Canada/Japan	Japanese periodicals and newspapers in Western languages; an international union list.
various	Union list of educational periodicals held by UNESCO libraries and documentation services.
Scandinavia	Nordisk samkatalog över periodica (NOSP).
various	Union list of medical periodicals published in the Southeast Asian countries.
Canada/U.S.	Union list of population/family planning periodicals.
various	Newspapers in microform.
Canada/U.S.	Union list of serials in libraries of the United States and Canada.
U.K./Eire	British union catalogue of periodicals.

Czechoslovakia/Austria/Hungary   Bibliografia slovenských novín
                                    a časopisov do roku 1918.

Section 2
Other Lists, Arranged Alphabetically by Country of Location of the Contributing Libraries

ARGENTINA

—Catálogo colectivo de publicaciones periódicas existentes en bibliotecas científicas y técnicas argentinas

AUSTRALIA

—Newspapers in Australian libraries
—Union list of Latin American serials in six Australian libraries
—Scientific serials in Australian Libraries (SSAL)
—Chinese periodicals in the libraries of the Australian National University, the University of Sydney, and the University of Melbourne
—Serials in Education in Australian Libraries
—Serials in Australian libraries: social sciences and humanities (SALSSAH)

AUSTRIA

—Zentralkatalog neuerer ausländischer Zeitschriften und Serien in Österreichischen Bibliotheken (ZAZ)

BELGIUM

—Répertoire des périodiques et grands traités de chimie et sciences connexes
—Environmental periodicals; Belgian union catalogue

BRAZIL

—Catálogo colectivo regional de periódicos, Bahia
—Catálogo colectivo de periódicos (Petróleo Brasileiro)

BULGARIA

—Chuzhdi periodichni izdaniĩa v po-golemite nauchni biblioteki
—Svoden katalog na periodichnite izdaniĩa po meditsina v po-golemite nauchni biblioteki v Bulgariĩa

CANADA

—Sheridan Park Association union list of serials
—Union list of serials in fine arts in Canadian libraries
—Union list of serials in Montreal health libraries
—Union list of Canadian newspapers held by Canadian libraries
—Union list of serials in Ontario government libraries
—Canadian locations of journals indexed for Medline
—Periodicals in Canadian law libraries; a union list
—Union list of scientific serials in Canadian libraries
—Saskatchewan union list of serials
—Union list of serials in the social sciences and humanities in Canadian libraries
—Central Vancouver Librarians' Group serials list
—Liste collective des publications périodiques des bibliothèques de la ville de Trois Rivières et des environs
—A.C.C.L. union list of serials
—Union list of serials in the Basilian libraries of the city of Toronto
—Historical directory of Nova Scotia newspapers and journals before Confederation

CHILE

—Catálogo colectivo de publicaciones periódicas del sector agropecuario y forestal
—Catálogo colectivo de publicaciones periódicas en ciencias biológicas y médicas existentes en las bibliotecas chilenas

CHINA (TAIWAN)

—Union list of Chinese periodicals in universities and colleges in Taiwan
—Union list of scientific serials in libraries of the Republic of China

COLOMBIA

—Catálogo colectivo nacional de publicaciones periódicas en tecnología y ciencias aplicadas

COSTA RICA

—Catálogo colectivo de publicaciones periódicas existentes en Costa Rica

CZECHOSLOVAKIA

—Soupis cizozemských periodik technických a příbuzných v knihovnách Československé republiky

EGYPT

—Union catalogue of scientific periodicals in Egypt

ETHIOPIA

—Combined catalogue of serials of the Addis Ababa University Libraries

FINLAND

—FINUC-S

FRANCE

—Catalogue collectif des périodiques du début du XVIIe siècle à 1939 conservés dans les bibliothèques de Paris et dans les bibliothèques universitaires
—2,000 revues d'Asie
—Catalogue collectif des journaux quotidiens d'information générale publiés en France métropolitaine de 1957 à 1961
—Périodiques slaves en caractères cyrilliques
—Inventaire des périodiques étrangers et des publications en série étrangères reçus en France par les bibliothèques et les organismes de documentation
—Liste des périodiques français et étrangers en cours conservés dans les bibliothèques et centres de documentation des départements: Tarn

GERMANY (EAST)

—Zeitschriftenzentralkatalog (ZZK)

GERMANY (WEST)

—Catalogue of foreign newspapers and illustrated papers in German libraries (SAZI)
—Zeitschriften-Datenbank (ZDB)

GREECE

—Union catalog of scientific periodicals in Greek libraries: Athens area

GUAM

—Union list of serials in libraries of Guam

HONG KONG

—Chinese University of Hong Kong University Library System union catalogue of serials

HUNGARY

—A Budapesti Műszaki Egyetem könyvtári hálózata folyóiratainak lelőhelyjegyzéke
—Központi címjegyzék a kémia és a vegyipar külföldi folyóiratairól

INDIA

—Periodicals in humanities (Delhi libraries)
—Regional union catalogue of scientific serials, Bombay-Poona

INDONESIA

—Check list of serials in Indonesian libraries
—Indonesian serials, 1942/50
—Katalog induk majalah

IRAN

—Iranian national union list of serials

ISRAEL

—Union list of abstracting and indexing services in special libraries in Israel
—Union list of serials in Israel libraries

ITALY

—Catalogo delle pubblicazioni periodiche esistenti in varie biblioteche di Roma e Firenze
—Union list of American periodicals in Italy
—Bibliografia dei periodici Toscani

IVORY COAST

—Périodiques spécialisés existant à Abidjan: essai de catalogue collectif

JAPAN

—Toshokan johogaku kankei gaikoko zasshi sogo mokuroku

KOREA

—Union catalogue of foreign scientific journals
—Union catalogue of periodicals, libraries of Ewha Woman's University, Sogang University and Yonsei University

KUWAIT

—Kuwait union list of scientific and technical periodicals

LIBYA

—Periodicals in Libya; a union list

MALTA

—Checklist of Maltese periodicals and newspapers in the National Library of Malta and the University of Malta Library

MEXICO

—Catálogo colectivo de publicaciones periódicas existentes en bibliotecas de la República Mexicana

NETHERLANDS

—Centrale catalogus van periodieken en seriewerken in nederlandse Bibliotheken (CCP)

NEW ZEALAND

—Check-list of classical periodicals in New Zealand libraries
—Union list of conference proceedings in New Zealand libraries
—Union list of serials in New Zealand libraries

NIGERIA

—Combined catalogue of serials of the Ahmadu Bello University Libraries
—Union list of scientific and technical periodicals in Nigerian libraries
—Union list of periodicals in member libraries (Lagos Special Libraries Information Service)
—National union list of serials in Nigerian libraries (NULOS)

NORWAY

—Norsk samkatalog. Utenlandske periodika i Norge (SAMKATPER)

PAKISTAN

—Union catalogue of scientific and technical periodicals in the libraries of Pakistan
—Union catalogue of social science periodicals of select libraries of Lahore

PAPUA NEW GUINEA

—National union list of serials held in Papua New Guinea libraries (NULOS)

PERU

—Catálogo colectivo de publicaciones periódicas en desarrollo económico y social

PHILIPPINES

—National union list of serials for science and technology

POLAND

—Centralny katalog czasopism zagranicznych w bibliotekach Łódzkich
—Centralny katalog bieżących czasopism zagranicznych w bibliotekach polskich

PORTUGAL

—Publicaçôes periódicas de interesse económico-social; catálogo

RHODESIA

—Periodicals in Rhodesian libraries

SAUDI ARABIA

—Union list of periodicals (non-Arabic)-Riyad University Libraries

SENEGAL

—Catalogue collectif des périodiques reçus à la bibliothèque de l'université et dans les autres bibliothèques de Dakar

SPAIN

—Inventario de publicaciones periódicas que se reciben en las bibliotecas de Barcelona
—Catálogo colectivo de publicaciones periódicas en bibliotecas españolas

SRI LANKA

—Union list of scientific periodicals in Ceylon

SUDAN

—Sudanese union-catalogue of periodicals

SWEDEN

—AKP
—Sovjetunionen 1917-1964; List of Soviet periodicals in the field of economics in Swedish libraries

SWITZERLAND

—Verzeichnis ausländischer Zeitschriften in schweizerischen Bibliotheken
—Biomed

TANZANIA

—Periodicals in Tanzania libraries; a union list

THAILAND

—Scientific serials in Thai libraries

U.S.S.R.

—Svodnyĭ katalog inostrannykh nauchnykh zhurnalov, postupivshikh v biblioteki SSSR
—Retrospektivnyĭ svodnyi ukazatel' inostrannykh periodicheskikh i prodolzhai͡ushchikhsi͡a izdaniĭ, imei͡ushikhsi͡a v krupneĭshikh bibliotekakh SSSR, 1750-1965
—Inostrannye periodicheskie izdanii͡a po bibliografii i bibliotekovedenii͡u, imei͡ushchiesi͡a v bibliotekakh Moskvy i Leningrada; svodnyi katalog, seredina XVII v. -1955 g.

UNITED KINGDOM

—Union list of serials in the science area, Oxford
—Chinese periodicals in British libraries
—World list of national newspapers
—Union list of Commonwealth newspapers in London, Oxford and Cambridge
—Union list of legal periodicals
—Union catalogue of the serial publications of the Indian government, 1858-1947
—Union list of statistical serials in British libraries
—University of London union list of serials
—Union list of periodicals on art and related subject fields
—Current serials available in the University Library and in other libraries connected with the University of Cambridge
—Periodicals from Africa
—Union list of periodicals in music in the library of the University of London and some other London libraries

—Union list of periodicals held in the libraries of Scottish colleges of education
—Latin American economic and social serials
—Essex union list of serials
—M.I.S.L.I.C. union list of periodicals
—London union list of periodicals (LULOP)
—Commonwealth literature periodicals
—Union catalogue of Arabic serials and newspapers in British libraries
—Union list of current periodicals in the libraries of the constituent colleges and schools of the University of Wales
—Union list of American historical periodicals in United Kingdom libraries

UNITED STATES

—Music school serials (Kentucky)
—Russian, Ukrainian and Belorussian newspapers, 1917-1953; a union list
—Union list of little magazines
—Union list of Arabic serials in the United States
—Guide to Wisconsin newspapers, 1833-1957
—Latin American newspapers in United States libraries
—Union list of serials for public utility libraries
—Minnesota union list of serials
—Union list of selected Pennsylvania serial documents
—California union list of periodicals
—Missouri union list of serial publications
—North Country union list of serials
—C.A.H.S.L.: union list of serials in health sciences libraries of Connecticut
—SERLINE
—Union listing of currently received newspapers (Chicago)
—King County Library System/Seattle Public Library union list of serials
—Union list of serials held by Seattle law firm libraries
—Union list of legal periodicals, Washington, D.C.
—Team-A serials
—Newspapers and periodicals by and about Black people: southeastern library holdings
—University of California union list of serials

URUGUAY

—Catálogo colectivo de publicaciones periódicas existentes en las bibliotecas universitarias del Uruguay

VENEZUELA

—Catálogo colectivo de publicaciones periódicas en las bibliotecas de la región centro occidental

YUGOSLAVIA

—Centralen katalog na stranskite periodični publikacii vo SR Makedonija

Index

References are to paragraph numbers in the *Guidelines* except where specified otherwise. Definitions of technical terms are found in the *Glossary and Abbreviations* (Appendix II, pp. 101-105), which is not indexed here.

AACR.2, pp. 2-3, 6.1.1, 6.1.2, 6.3.3.1 and ISDS standard, p. 8
ABBREVIATIONS AND ACRONYMS (USED IN TEXT), Appendix II, pp. 104-105
ABBREVIATIONS FOR SERIAL TITLES, 6.3.3.2, 8.1.1, 8.1.3
ACCESS POINTS, 1.2.1, 3.3, 6.3.2, 6.3.3.2
  commercial publishers' names, 12.6
  corporate body, 2.4, 6.3.2, 6.3.3.2, 8.1.3, 8.1.4, 8.1.5, 9.2, 9.7.2, 9.7.3.1, 9.7.4
  documents classification nos., 12.6
  geographic area, 6.3.3.3, 9.1, 9.1.3, 9.2, 9.5, 9.7.3, 11.5
  ISSN, 2.4, 6.1.4, 8.1.4, 8.1.5, 9.7.4, 11.2
  intellectual level, 11.4
  key words and phrases, 9.7.3, 9.7.4, 11.2
  language, 9.5, 9.7.3, 11.6
  local control nos., 7.4.4
  national bibliography nos., 6.3.3, 9.2, 9.7.4, 11.2
  newspapers, 9.1
  stock control nos., 12.6
  subject, 8.1.6, 9.4, 9.5, 9.7.3.1, 9.7.4, 11.2
ACQUISITION, 2.1
  co-operative, p. 8, 1.2.3, 2, 2.1, 2.7, 4.3.2, 4.3.3, 8.1.6, 9.4
  of government publications, 9.2
  use of holdings statements, p. 3, p. 8, 2.1, 2.3
  of newspapers, 9.1, 9.1.4
  use of numbering systems for ordering serials, 12.6
  of older serials, 9.5
  ordering data in serials directories, 12.5
  subject selection, 8.1.6
ACRONYMS (USED IN TEXT). *See* ABBREVIATIONS AND ACRONYMS
ANGLO-AMERICAN CATALOGUING RULES. See *AACR.2*
ANSI (AMERICAN NATIONAL STANDARDS INSTITUTE)
  holdings standard, p. 3
AUTHORITY FILES, 6.2
  role of contributing libraries, 10.2.1
  for geographic names, 4.2.1, 9.1.3
  for uniform titles, 4.2.1, 6.2
  in union catalogue agency, 5.2.2, 10.1.1

BSI (BRITISH STANDARDS INSTITUTION)
  holdings standard, p. 3
BIBLIOGRAPHIC CONTROL, 6-6.7. *See also* AUTHORITY FILES; CATALOGUING OF NEWSPAPERS; CATALOGUING OF SERIALS
  cataloguing policies, 8.1.1, 10.1.1
  role of contributing libraries, p. 8, 10.2.1
  data elements in union catalogues, 6.3-6.4.4; summary of, Appendix III, pp. 107-108
  data sources, 1.2.1, 4.4, 5.1-5.2.4, 6.3.3.1, 6.7, 12.1.2
  full and mini records, 5.2.2, 6.3-6.3.3.3, 9.7.2
  relationship of bibliographic and holdings data, 2, 6.3.1-6.3.3, 6.5.3, 6.5.4, 7.2, 7.7.3
  standards and standardization, p. 3, p. 9, 5.2.2, 5.2.4, 6.1.1-6.7, 8.1.1, 10.1.1, 12.9
  use of union catalogue of serials in, 2.4-2.5
BIBLIOGRAPHIC LEVELS
  in fullness of serials cataloguing, p. 8, 5.2.2, 6.3-6.3.3.1, 6.3.3.3, 8.1.5, 9.7.2
  types and relationships, 12.2
BIBLIOGRAPHIC UTILITIES, p. 3, p. 8, 1.2.1, 5.1
BOOLEAN LOGIC OPERATORS, 9.7.3
BRITISH STANDARDS INSTITUTION. *See* BSI

CRT TERMINALS
  safety standards, 3.3.1
CANADIAN UNION CATALOGUE TASK GROUP
  holdings standard, p. 3, 5.2.3, 7.2
CATALOGUING CODES, 6.1.1, 10.1.1. See also *AACR.2*
  ISBD(S), p. 8, 6.1.2
  ISDS, p. 9, 6.1.4
  and microforms, 6.6-6.6.1.1
  and newspapers, p. 9, 9.1
  RAK, 6.1.1, 6.1.2
  Uniform Rules, 6.1.1
  User knowledge of, 9.7.3.1
CATALOGUING OF NEWSPAPERS, p. 9, 6.5.1.1, 6.6, 9.1, 9.1.1, 9.1.3
CATALOGUING OF SERIALS, 6-6.7
  central serials records as source of data for, 12.1.2
  co-operative, 5.1-5.2.2, 5.2.4, 6.3.2, 10.2.1
  government publications, 9.2
  ISBD(S) level of, p. 8, 6.1.2, 6.3
  ISDS level of, 6.1.4
  key-titles in, 6.1.4, 6.4.4
  microforms, 6.3.2, 6.3.3, 6.6-6.6.2
  role of national bibliographic agency in, 4.2.1
  in non-Roman scripts, 6.7
  reprints, 6.3.2, 6.3.3, 6.6.1.2-6.6.2
  subject, 8.1.6, 9.7.1.1

successive-entry, 6.5-6.5.4, 9.1.1, 9.7.2
uniform titles in, 4.2.1, 6.2, 6.3.3, 6.4-6.4.4
union catalogue of serials as source of bibliographic data for, 2.4; as context for new, 2.4
user knowledge of practices in, 8.1.1
CENTRAL SERIALS RECORDS, 12.1-12.1.2
CITATIONS
commercial publishers, names used in, 12.6
correspondence with entries in union catalogues, 7.4.2.2, 8.1.3
imprecise, solutions to, 2.4, 8.1.3, 9.7.3.1
to monographic series, 12.2.1
to newspapers, 7.4.2, 9.1, 12.6
in on-line literature searches, 2.6, 12.4
to serial documents, 7.4.2
and successive-entry cataloguing, 6.5.1
as user approach to periodical literature, 8.1.6
COM (COMPUTER-OUTPUT-MICROFORM). *See also* MICROFORMS
as bibliography, 9.6-9.6.1
catalogues, 11.2
formats, 3.2, 3.4, 3.5, 9.6.1
identification of, 9.6.1
standards for, 9.6-9.6.1
and user education, 3.2, 9.6.1, 10.1.1
COMMON COMMUNICATION FORMAT, p. 9, 5.2
COMPUTER-OUTPUT-MICROFORM. *See* COM
CONCORDANCES, CHRONOLOGICAL, 12.8
CONFERENCE PROCEEDINGS, 9.3
CONSER (CONVERSION OF SERIALS PROJECT)
holdings standard, p. 3
as source of bibliographic data for union catalogues, 5.1, 5.2.4
as union catalogue data base, p. 3
CO-OPERATIVE PROGRAMMES FOR SERIALS
acquisition, p. 8, 1.2.3, 2, 2.1, 2.7, 4.3.2, 4.3.3, 8.1.6, 9.1, 9.4
cataloguing, 5.1-5.2.2, 5.2.4, 9.2
preservation, 2.3

DATE SYSTEMS IN HOLDINGS CONTROL, 7.2, 7.3, 7.4.2, 7.4.2.2
DEVELOPING COUNTRIES
and computerization, p.3
funding needs for union catalogues, p. 10
handbook for serials control, p. 10
serials published in, 4.4
use of union catalogues, 2.2, 2.6
DIRECTORIES
of contributors to union catalogues, 7.4.1, 8.1.1
of libraries, 12.7
of serials, p. 3, 12.5

ETHNIC NEWSPAPERS, 9.1, 9.1.2
ETHNIC SERIALS, 4.3.2
FILING SYSTEMS, 6.3.3.2, 6.4.3, 8.1.1, 8.1.2
FINUC-S (FINNISH UNION CATALOGUE-SERIALS), p. 8
GLOSSARY OF SIGNIFICANT TERMS (USED IN TEXT), Appendix II, pp. 101–104
GOVERNMENT PUBLICATIONS
  acquisition of, 9.2
  bibliographic control of, 9.2
  documents classification nos. as access point, 12.6
  holdings statements for, 7.4.2
  types of, 9.2
  in union catalogues, 4.3.2, 4.3.3, 4.4, 8.1.3, 9.2

HOLDINGS CONTROL, 7-7.7
  as by-product of local system, 7.2
  in central serials records, 12.1.1, 12.1.2
  chronological data, 7.2, 7.3, 7.4, 7.4.2, 7.4.2.2
  role of contributing libraries, 10.2.4
  correlation of chronological and numerical data, 12.8
  data elements in union catalogues, 6.3.2-6.3.3, 7.4-7.5;
  summary of, Appendix III, pp. 107-108
  data sources, 4.4, 5.2.5, 10.2.3, 12.1.2
  editing by union catalogue agency, p. 3, p. 8, 11.3
  examples of holdings statements, 7.7
  in historical bibliographies, 3.5, 9.5
  in institutional files, 11.3
  institutional symbols, 7.3, 7.4, 7.4.1
  in on-line displays, 3.3, 9.7.2
  for microforms, 2.3, 7.2, 7.3, 7.4.2.3, 7.4.3, 6.6.1.1
  for monographic series, 12.2.1
  for newspapers, 2.3, 3.5, 7.4.1, 7.4.2, 7.4.2.2, 7.4.3, 9.1, 9.1.4
  numerical data, 7.2, 7.3, 7.4, 7.4.2, 7.4.2.1
  principles of, 7.3
  punctuation conventions and abbreviations, 7.4.2.1, 7.4.2.3, 7.6
  in register-index format, 8.1.5
  relationship of bibliographic and holdings data, 2, 6.3.1-6.3.3, 6.5.3-6.5.4, 7.2, 7.7.3
  retention statements, 7.2, 7.4, 7.4.2.3
  standards and standardization, p. 3, p. 8, p. 9, 5.2.3, 7-7.2, 10.1.1, 12.9
  for translation journals, 7.3
  and user education, 8.1.1
  uses of holdings statements, p. 3, p. 8, 2.1, 2.2, 2.3

ISBD(S) (INTERNATIONAL STANDARD BIBLIOGRAPHIC DESCRIPTION FOR SERIALS), p. 8, 6.1.2
ISDS (INTERNATIONAL SERIALS DATA SYSTEM), 4.4, 6.1.4
  and *AACR.2*, p. 8

definition of serial, 4.1
Guidelines for ISDS, 6.4.4
and national bibliographic agencies, 4.2.1
and newspapers, p. 9
romanization standard, 6.7
and serials in microform and reproduction, p. 9
as source of bibliographic data for union catalogues, 5.1
as union catalogue data base, p. 3, pp. 7-8
ISSN (INTERNATIONAL STANDARD SERIAL NUMBER)
as access point to on-line systems, 9.7.4
functions of, 6.1.4
indexes, 8.1.4, 8.1.5, 9.7.4, 11.2
in microfiche headers, 9.6.1
for monographic series, 12.2.1
on printed union catalogues, 8.1
for titles prior to 1960, p. 10
use of in union catalogues, pp. 7-8, 1.3, 2.4, 2.6, 4.2.1, 4.4, 5.2.4
IFLA (INTERNATIONAL FEDERATION OF LIBRARY ASSOCIATIONS
AND INSTITUTIONS)
annual conference: 1978 (Czechoslovakia), p. 2
annual conference: 1979 (Copenhagen), p. 4
annual conference: 1981 (Leipzig), p. 6
objectives, p. 1
organization and programmes, p. 1
relationship with UNESCO, p. 1
Section on Serial Publications, p. 1, pp. 9–11; Working Group on Newspapers,
   p. 9; Working Group on Union Catalogues of Serials, p. 9, p. 10
standards, 6.1.2, 11.4
INDEXES
corporate body, 3.5, 6.3.3.2, 8.1.3, 8.1.4, 8.1.5, 9.7.2, 11.2
geographic, 6.3.3.2
ISSN, 6.3.3.2, 8.1.4, 8.1.5, 9.7.4, 11.2
key words and phrases, 9.7.3, 9.7.4, 11.2
in microfiche editions, 9.6.1
subject, 8.1.5
title, 6.3.3.2, 8.1.5, 9.2, 9.7.2, 9.7.4
title and place of publication, 9.1.5
and user education, 8.1.1
INDEXING AND ABSTRACTING SERVICES
bibliographies of titles covered by, 11.2
coverage data in serials directories, 12.5
links with union catalogues, 2.6, 5.2.1, 12.4
subject access in, 8.1.6
and title access in union catalogues, 8.1.3
as union catalogue data bases, p. 3
INTER-LIBRARY-LOAN
agreements, 1.2.3
automated requests, 2.6, 5.2.1, 5.2.3, 7.4.4

CRT problems, 3.3.1
as criterion in UNESCO/IFLA international survey, p. 6
use of holdings statements, p. 4, p. 8, 4.3.2, 4.3.3, 7.3, 7.4.1
loan and photocopying policies, 8.1.1
microfiche problems, 3.2
national and international systems of, p. 7, 2.2, 2.6, 4.2, 4.2.1, 4.3.4
newspapers, 9.1.4
on-line services, 2.6, 3.3, 3.3.2, 5.2.1, 12.4
patron interface, 3.3.2
"speculative" requests, 6.3.2
and subject searches, 9.4
use of union catalogues in, 2, 2.2, 2.6
INTERNATIONAL FEDERATION OF LIBRARY ASSOCIATIONS AND INSTITUTIONS. See IFLA
INTERNATIONAL ORGANIZATION FOR STANDARDIZATION. See ISO
INTERNATIONAL SERIALS DATA SYSTEM. See ISDS
INTERNATIONAL STANDARD BIBLIOGRAPHIC DESCRIPTION FOR SERIALS. See ISBD(S)
INTERNATIONAL STANDARD SERIAL NUMBER. See ISSN
INTERNATIONAL TARGET AUDIENCE CODE. See ITAC
ISO (INTERNATIONAL ORGANIZATION FOR STANDARDIZATION)
country code (ISO 3166), 11.5
format for bibliographic information interchange on magnetic tape (ISO 2709), 5.2.1
holdings standard, p. 9
language code (ISO 639), 11.6
micrographics standards, p. 10, 9.6.1
romanization systems, 6.7
standard serial number (ISO 3297), 6.1.4
ITAC (INTERNATIONAL TARGET AUDIENCE CODE), 11.4

KEY WORDS AND PHRASES
indexes, 11.2
in on-line systems, 9.7, 9.7.3, 9.7.4
as subject approach, 8.1.6, 9.7.3.1, 9.7.4

LIBRARY OF CONGRESS
codes, 11.5
MARC format, 5.2.1
LOAN AND PHOTOCOPYING POLICIES, 8.1.1

MACHINE-READABLE SERIALS DATA BASES, 5.1-5.2.4
bibliography-building capabilities, 5.2.1, 5.2.4, 11.2
compatibility, 5.2.4, 10.2.3
government publications, 9.2
"master" files, p. 3, 5.1, 5.2.4
newspapers, 9.1.2
on-line, 3.3-3.3.2, 9.7-9.7.4
products and by-products, 8.1.1, 11

searching, 3.3.2, 8.1.6, 9.7-9.7.4, 11.2
up-dating capabilities, 3.5
MARC FORMAT(S)
Canadian, 5.2.2, 5.2.3, 7.2, p. 95 References (8)
and compatibility of files, 1.2.1, 10.2.3
Library of Congress, 5.2.1
for newspapers, p. 95 References (8)
and period bibliographies, 9.5
for serials, 1.2.1, 5.1, 5.2.2, 5.2.4
UNIMARC, 5.2.1
MICROFORMS. *See also* COM
bibliographies, 11.2
cataloguing of, p. 9, 6.3.2, 6.3.3, 6.6-6.6.2
holdings statements for, 7.2, 7.3, 7.4.3, 7.4.2.3
repositories of masters, 9.1.4
newspapers in, 6.6, 9.1, 9.1.1, 9.1.4
MONOGRAPHIC SERIES
citations, 12.2.1
control of serial and monographic aspects, 12.2.1
subject access, 8.1.6

NATIONAL BIBLIOGRAPHIC AGENCY
cataloguing in original scripts, 6.7
as compiler of union catalogues, 4.2.1, 5.1-5.2.1, 5.2.4
depository for published union catalogues, p. 10, 10.1.1, 11.1
and ISDS cataloguing, p. 8
serials collections, 2.3, 4.3.4
symbols assigned to union catalogue contributors, 7.4.1
NATIONAL BIBLIOGRAPHIES
coverage of government serials, 4.3.2, 9.1.5; of local serials, 4.3.2; of newspapers, 4.3.2, 9.1
in register-index format, 8.1.5
as source of union catalogue data, 1.2.1, 6.1.3, 6.3.3.1, 6.3.3.3, 6.7, 12.3
union catalogue as substitute for serials data in, 2.3, 2.4, 2.5, 12.3
use of control numbers, 6.3.3, 9.7.4
NATIONAL LENDING COLLECTIONS, 2.2, 4.2, 4.3.3, 12.3
NEWSPAPERS
acquisition of, 9.1.4
arrangement in union catalogue, 8.1.3, 9.1, 9.1.1, 9.1.3, 9.1.5
bibliographies, 2.5, 9.1.2, 9.5
cataloguing problems, p. 9, 6.5.1.1, 6.6, 9.1, 9.1.1, 9.1.3
contributors to union catalogues of, 1.2.3, 7.4.1
definition of, 4.1, 9.1, 9.1.1, 9.1.2
early, 9.5
ethnic, 9.1, 9.1.2
holdings statements for, 2.3, 3.5, 7.4.2, 7.4.2.1, 7.4.3, 9.1, 9.1.4
IFLA Working Group on, p. 9
inventory of, 2.3

in MARC format(s), p. 95 References (8)
in microform, 6.6, 9.1, 9.1.1, 9.1.4
preservation of, 2.3
publishing patterns, 9.1
in separate systems, 4.4, 9.1, 12.2
suppressed, 9.5
NOSP (NORDISK SAMKATALOG ÖVER PERIODICA-UNION CATALOGUE OF SERIALS IN NORDIC RESEARCH LIBRARIES), p. 8, p. 11
NUMBERING SYSTEMS IN HOLDINGS CONTROL, 7.2, 7.3, 7.4.2, 7.4.2.1

OSI (OPEN SYSTEMS INTERCONNECTION)
 chronological concordances to be made available through, 12.8
 planning for, p. 2
 technological developments and standardization, *Guidelines* Introduction p. 16, 12, 12.9
ON-LINE SERVICES AND SYSTEMS
 access points, 3.3, 3.3.2, 9.7, 9.7.3, 9.7.4
 advantages and capabilities of, 2.4, 2.6, 3.3, 3.5, 5.2.1, 6.3.3.3, 6.5.4, 8.1.6, 9.7, 9.7.3
 link between patron and serial material required, 2.6, 3.3.2, 5.2.1, 12.4
 as method of input to union catalogue, 1.2.1, 3.3, 10.2.2
 and non-Roman scripts, 6.7
 safety standards, 3.3.1
 searching of union catalogues, 2.6, 3.3, 3.3.2, 9.7-9.7.4; by geographic area, 9.7.3; by language, 9.7.3; by medium, 9.7.3; by period, 9.5, 9.7.3; by subject, 8.1.6
 as source of directory data, 8.1.1, 12.5
 and user education, 3.3.2, 9.7.1.1-9.7.1.2, 10.1.1

PRECIS, 8.1.6
PRICES OF SERIALS, 12.5
PUBLISHERS OF SERIALS
 commercial publishers' names as access points, 12.6
 confiscated firms, 9.5
 of government serials, 9.2
 of newspapers, 1.2.3, 7.4.1
 as source of acquisition data, 12.5
 as source of chronological concordance data, 12.8
 use of lists and catalogues of, 12.6
 use of numbering systems, 12.6

REGISTER-INDEX FORMAT, 8.1.5
ROMANIZATION SYSTEMS, 6.7, 8.1.1, 8.1.2

SCRIPTS, NON-ROMAN, 6.7, 8.1.2, 8.1.3
SERIAL
 Definition of, 1.1.1, 4.1, Appendix I p. 99
SERIALS. *See also* CONFERENCE PROCEEDINGS, GOVERNMENT

PUBLICATIONS, MONOGRAPHIC SERIES, NEWSPAPERS, TECHNICAL REPORTS
SERIALS
  Types of, Appendix I pp. 99-100
SERIALS BIBLIOGRAPHIES, 2.5
  as by-products of union catalogue, 2.5, 11.2
  corporate body, 8.1.3, 8.1.5, 9.2, 9.7.2, 9.7.3, 9.7.4
  critical titles, 11.2
  geographic area, 8.1.3, 9.1, 9.1.3, 9.2, 9.5, 9.7.3, 11.5
  historical, 9.5
  intellectual level, 11.4
  international, 4.3.5
  language, 9.5, 9.7.3, 11.6
  local, 4.3.2
  microfiche as, 9.6-9.6.1
  microform masters, 11.2
  national, 4.3.4, 12.3
  new serial titles, 11.2
  newspapers, 2.5, 9.1.2, 9.5
  period, 9.5, 9.7.3
  regional, 4.3.3
  selective, 11.2
  subject, 8.1.6, 9.4, 9.5, 9.7.3.1, 9.7.4, 11.2
  titles covered by indexing and abstracting services, 11.2
SERIALS CATALOGUES
  institutional, 1.1.2, 2.4, 4.3.1, 10.2.3, 11.3
SERIALS COLLECTIONS
  access to, 2.2, 2.4
  development of, 2.1
  preservation of, 2.3
  utilization of, 2.6
SERIALS DEPARTMENTS
  organization and functions, 10.2
SERIALS DIRECTORIES, p. 3, 12.5
SERIALS MANAGEMENT SYSTEMS, p. 3, 7.2, 10.2.3
SERIALS NETWORKS, 2.6, 4.2
STANDARDS AND STANDARDIZATION, 1.3, 1.5
  abbreviations for serial titles, 8.1.3
  bibliographic data, p. 3, p. 9, 4.2.1, 5.2.2, 6.1.1-4, 6.7, 10.1.1, 12.9
  CRT terminals, 3.3.1
  cataloguing codes, 6.1.1
filing systems, 8.1.2
  holdings data, 5.2.3, 7-7.2, 10.1.1, 12.9; ANSI, p. 3
    BSI, p. 3, CONSER, p. 3; Canadian, p. 3, 5.2.3, 7.2; need for international, p. 3, pp. 8-9
  ISDS, 1.3, 4.2.1, 6.1.4
  ISO, 5.2.1, 6.1.4, 9.6.1, 11.5, 11.6
  Library of Congress, 11.5

location data, p. 9, 12.9
microfiche, p. 10, 9.6-9.6.1
role of national bibliographic agency, 4.2.1
for OSI, 12.9
romanization systems, 6.7
subject, 8.1.6
and user education, 8.1.1
SUBJECT CATALOGUES, 8.1.6
　as by-products of union catalogue, 4.4, 11.2
　and historical bibliographies, 9.5
　and newspapers, 9.1.3
　and on-line systems, 9.7.1.1, 9.7.3.1, 9.7.4

TECHNICAL REPORTS
　use of stock numbers, 12.6
TRANSLATION JOURNALS, 7.3

UAP (UNIVERSAL AVAILABILITY OF PUBLICATIONS)
　contribution of international union catalogues to, 4.3.5
　and hierarchical national lending system, p. 7
　objectives, p. 2
　standards as contribution to, 5.2.3, 12.9
　and UNESCO/IFLA Union List Project, p. 2
　role of union catalogues in, 2.2
UBC (UNIVERSAL BIBLIOGRAPHIC CONTROL)
　objectives, p. 2, 4.2.1
　standards as contribution to, 5.2.3, 6.1.2, 12.9
　and UNESCO/IFLA Union List Project, p. 2
UNESCO (UNITED NATIONS EDUCATIONAL, SCIENTIFIC AND CULTURAL ORGANIZATION)
　and funds for developing countries, p. 10
　guidelines series, p. 11
　relationship with IFLA, pp. 1-2
　UBC programme, p. 2, 4.2.1
　UNISIST programme, 6.1.4
UNESCO/IFLA UNION LIST PROJECT
　history, pp. 1-11
　Guidelines for Union Catalogues of Serials, objectives and value, *Guidelines* Introduction pp. 15-16
　international survey, pp. 3-6, *Guidelines* Introduction p. 15; list of titles covered by, Supplement pp. 109-125
　results and recommendations, pp. 7-10
　methodology, pp. 3-6
　objectives, p. 2
　realization in *Guidelines,* p. 6, p. 10
　and UAP programme, p. 2
　and UBC programme, p. 2

UNION CATALOGUES OF SERIALS
— area of contribution, 1.1.2, 4, 4.2-4.4, 7.3; international, 4.3.5; local, 4.3.2, 7.3; national, 4.3.2, 4.3.3, 4.3.4, 7.3; regional, 4.3.2, 4.3.3; single library system, 1.1.2, 4.3.1; as factor in method of compilation, 5.1
— arrangement, 8-8.4, 10.1.1; filing systems, 8.1.1, 8.1.2; government publications, 9.2; historical bibliographies, 9.5; holdings statements, 7.3, 7.4, 7.4.1; microfiche catalogues, 9.6.1; newspapers, 9.1, 9.1.1, 9.1.3, 9.1.5; non-Roman scripts, 6.7, 8.1.2, 8.1.3; register-index format, 8.1.5
— authenticating centres, 10.2.1
— bibliographic control *See* BIBLIOGRAPHIC CONTROL
— clearinghouses, p. 10; union catalogues as, 2.6
— co-operative venture, 1.2-1.5, 2.6, 5.2.4, 10
— compilation, methods of, p. 8, 5.1-5.2.5, 10.2.2-10.2.3
— contributors, directory information concerning, 8.1.1; loan and photocopying policies, 8.1.1; responsibilities of, p. 8, 7.1, 10.2-10.2.4; symbols of, p. 9, 7.3, 7.4.1, 8.1.1; training and instruction, 10.1.1; to union catalogues of newspapers, 1.2.3, 9.1.4
— definition of, 1.1.2
— editorial office, 1.2.2, 1.3; policies, 8.1.1; as publisher, 11.1; responsibilities of, p. 3, p. 8, 1.5, 4, 5.1, 7.1, 7.3, 10.1-10.1.1, 10.2.1, 11.3
— formats, display in on-line systems, 3.3, 3.3.2, 3.4, 3.5, 9.7.2; machine-readable design, 12.4; microfiche, 3.2, 3.4, 3.5, 9.6.1; print, 3.1, 3.2, 3.4, 3.5; register-index, 8.1.5
— functions, 2-2.6, 8.1.1; re-defined in *Guidelines,* p. 6; as directory of libraries, 12.7; evaluated in international survey, p. 6; of historical bibliographies, p. 6, 9.5; of holdings statements, p. 3, p. 8, 2.1, 2.2, 2.3; compared with national bibliography, 12.3; additional in on-line systems, 2.4, 3.3, 9.7-9.7.4; as subject bibliographies, 8.1.6, 9.4; and UAP programme, p. 2, 2.2; of union catalogues of newspapers, 9.1
— holdings control *See* HOLDINGS CONTROL
— interface with other systems of serials control, 2.6, 5.2.4, 12; central serials records, 12.1; chronological concordances, 12.8; directories of libraries, 12.7; directories of serials, 12.5; information transfer chain and OSI, 2.6, 5.2.1, 6.1.4, 12.9; indexing and abstracting services, 2.6, 5.2.1, 12.4; monographic data banks, 10.1.1, 12.2; national bibliography, 12.3; publishers' lists and catalogues, 12.6; publishers' numbering systems, 12.6; serials management systems, 2.4, 6.6.1-6.6.1.1; of different levels of union catalogues, 4, 4.2-4.3.5
— location data, in register-index formats, 8.1.5; symbols of contributors, p. 8, 7.3, 7.4-7.4.1, 8.1.1; standardization, need for, 7.4.1, 12.9
— products and by-products, 4.2, 4.4, 11.1-11.6; geographic area, 9.7.3; language, 9.7.3; newspaper bibliographies, 9.1.2; on-line capabilities, 9.7.3; period bibliographies, 9.5, 9.7.3; subject catalogues, 9.4; and user education, 8.1.1
— project director, responsibilities of, 1.2.1, 1.2.3, 3.5, 5.1
— publication and distribution, 1.2.2, 3.1, 3.2, 3.3, 8.1, 10.1.1, 11.1
— scope, 4-4.4, 8.1, 8.1.1, 12, 12.2.1; historical, 9.5; newspapers, 9.1.1; subject, 9.4
— staffing, in institutions contributing to union catalogues, p. 8, 1.2.3, 7.1, 9.1, 10.2, 10.2.4; in union catalogue agencies, p. 8, 1.2.1-1.3, 7.1, 9.1, 10.1-10.1.1

— systems design, 5.1-5.2.4, 6.5.4, 7.4.4-7.4.5, 9.1.2, 10.1.1, 11.2; in on-line systems, 3.3.2, 9.5, 9.7-9.7.4
— types, conference proceedings, 9.3; government publications, 9.2; historical bibliographies, 3.5, 9.5; international, 4.3.5; law, 9.4; local, 4.3.2; microfiche, 3.2, 3.4, 3.5, 9.6-9.6.1; music, 9.4; national, 4.3.4; newspapers, p. 9, 1.2.3, 3.5, 9-9.1.5; on-line, 3.3-3.3.2, 9.7-9.7.4; regional, 4.3.3; single institution, 4.3.1; subject bibliographies, 9.4
— up-dating, 1.2.2, 3.1, 3.2, 3.3, 3.5, 9.1.4, 9.5
— user education, 3.2, 8.1.1, 9.6.1, 10.1.1; for on-line systems, 3.3.2, 9.7.1.1-9.7.1.2, 10.1.1
UNION LISTS OF SERIALS, p. 9, 1
UNITED NATIONS EDUCATIONAL, SCIENTIFIC AND CULTURAL ORGANIZATION. *See* UNESCO
UNIVERSAL AVAILABILITY OF PUBLICATIONS. *See* UAP
UNIVERSAL BIBLIOGRAPHIC CONTROL. *See* UBC